CAMP GRUB

A CLASSIC HANDBOOK ON OUTDOORS COOKING
AND HAVING DELICIOUS MEALS IN CAMP AND ON
THE TRAIL

BY **ELON JESSUP**

ORIGINALLY PUBLISHED IN 1924

LEGACY EDITION

THE LIBRARY OF AMERICAN OUTDOORS CLASSICS

FEATURING

REMASTERED CLASSIC WORKS OF THE HIGHEST
QUALITY FROM **THE TIMELESS MASTERS AND
TEACHERS** OF TRADITIONAL HANDCRAFTS AND
OUTDOORS SKILLS

Doublebit Press

New content, introduction, cover design, and annotations Copyright © 2021 by Doublebit Press. All rights reserved. www.doublebitpress.com | Cherry, IL, USA. First published in 1924 by Elon Jessup.

Doublebit Press Legacy Edition ISBNs Hardcover: 978-1-64389-186-6 Paperback: 978-1-64389-187-3

WARNING: Some of the material in this book may be outdated by modern safety standards. This antique text may contain outdated and unsafe recreational activities, cooking, projects, or mechanical, electrical, chemical, or medical practices. Use of this book may result in unsafe and hazardous conditions and individuals act at their own risk and are responsible for their own safety. Doublebit Press, its authors, or its agents assume no liability for any injury, harm, or damages to persons or property arising either directly or indirectly from any content contained in this text or the activities performed by readers. Remember to be safe with any activity or work you do and follow proper health and safety protocols. In addition, because this book was from a past time and is presented in an unabridged form, the contents may be culturally or racially insensitive. Such content does not represent the opinions or positions of the publisher and are presented for historical posterity and accuracy to the original text.

DISCLAIMER: Doublebit Press has not tested or analyzed the methods, materials, and practices appearing in this public domain text and provides no warranty to the accuracy and reliability of the content. This text is provided only as a reprinted facsimile from the unedited public domain original as first published and authored. This text is published for historical study and personal literary enrichment purposes only and should only be used for such. The publisher assumes no liability for any injury, harm, or damages to persons or property arising either directly or indirectly from any information contained in this public domain book or activities performed by readers.

INTRODUCTION
To The Doublebit Press Legacy Edition

The old experts of the woods, mountains, and farm country life taught timeless principles and skills for decades. Through their books, the old experts offered rich descriptions of the outdoor world and encouraged learning through personal experiences in nature. Over the last 125 years, handcrafts, artisanal works, outdoors activities, and our experiences with nature have substantially changed. Many things have gotten simpler as equipment and processes have improved, and life outside, on the farm, or on the trail now brings with it many of the same comforts enjoyed in town. In addition, some activities of the old days are now no longer in vogue, or are even outright considered inappropriate or illegal. However, despite many of the positive changes in handcrafting, traditional skills, and outdoors methods that have occurred over the years, *there are many other skills and much knowledge that are at risk of being lost* that should never be forgotten.

By publishing Legacy Editions of classic texts on handcrafts, artisanal skills, nature lore, survival, and outdoors and camping life, it is our goal at Doublebit Press to do what we can to preserve and share the works from forgotten teachers that form the cornerstone of the authentic and hard-wrought American tradition of self-sustainability and self-reliance. Through remastered reprint editions of timeless classics of traditional crafts, classic methods, and outdoor recreation, perhaps we can regain some of this lost knowledge for future generations.

On the frontier, folks made virtually everything by hand. Old farmers' knowledge and homestead skills were passed on to the future generation because it meant survival. In addition, much of traditional handcrafts and outdoors life knowledge was passed on from American Indians – the original handcrafters and outdoorsmen of the Americas.

Today, much of the handcrafted items of the frontier are made in factories, only briefly seeing a human during the process (if at all). Making things by hand indeed takes much (often strenuous) work, but it provides an extreme sense of pride in the finished job. Instantly, all hand-made items come with a story on their creation. Most importantly, though, making items with traditional methods gives you experience and knowledge of how things work.

This is similar to the case of camping and the modern outdoors experience, with neatly arranged campsites at public campgrounds and camping gear that has been meticulously improved and tested in both the lab and the field. These changes have also caused us to lose this traditional knowledge, having it buried in the latest high-tech iteration of your latest camp gadget.

Many modern conveniences are only a brief trek away, with many parks, campgrounds, and even forests having easy-access roads, convenience stores, and even cell phone signal. In some ways, it is much easier to camp and go outdoors today, and that is a good thing! We should not be miserable when we go outside — lovers of the outdoors know the essential restorative capability that the woods can have on the body, mind, and soul. But to experience it, you need to not be surrounded by modern high-tech robotic coffee pots, tents that build themselves, or watches that tell you how to do everything!

Although things have gotten easier on us in the 21st Century when it comes to handcrafts and the outdoors, it certainly does not mean that we should forget the foundations of technical skills, artisanal production, and outdoors lore. All of the modern tools and cool gizmos that make our lives easier are all founded on principles of traditional methods that the old masters knew well and taught to those who would listen. We just have to look deeply into the design of our modern gadgets and factories to see the original methods and traditional skills at play.

Every woods master and artisan had their own curriculum or thought some things were more important than others. The old masters also taught common things in slightly different ways or did things differently than others. That's what makes each of the experts different and worth reading. There's no universal way of doing something, especially today. Learning to go about something differently helps with mastery or learn a new skill altogether. Basically, you learn intimately how things work, giving you great skill with adapting and being flexible when the need arises.

Again, to use the metaphor from the above paragraphs, traditional skills mastery consists of learning the basic building blocks of how and why the old artisans made things, how they lived outdoors, and why woods and nature lore mattered. Everything is intertwined, and doing it by hand increases your knowledge of this complex network. Each master goes about describing these building blocks differently or shows a different aspect of them.

Therefore, we have decided to publish this Legacy Edition reprint in our collection of traditional handcraft and outdoors life classics. This book is an important contribution to the early American traditional skills and outdoors literature, and has important historical and collector value toward preserving the American tradition of self-sufficiency and artisan production. The knowledge it holds is an invaluable reference for practicing outdoors skills and hand craft methods. Its chapters thoroughly discuss some of the essential building blocks of knowledge that are fundamental but may have been forgotten as equipment gets fancier and technology gets smarter. In short, this book was chosen for Legacy Edition printing because much of the basic skills and knowledge it contains has been forgotten or put to the wayside in trade for more modern conveniences and methods.

Although the editors at Doublebit Press are thrilled to have comfortable experiences in the woods and love our modern equipment for making cool hand-made projects, we are also realizing that the basic skills taught by the old masters are more essential than ever as our culture becomes more and more hooked on digital stuff. We don't want to risk forgetting the important steps, skills, or building blocks involved with each step of traditional methods. Sometimes, *there's no substitute for just doing something on your own, by hand.* Sometimes, to truly learn something is to *just do it by hand.* The Legacy Edition series represents the essential contributions to the American handcraft and outdoors tradition by the great experts.

With technology playing a major role in everyday life, sometimes we need to take a step back in time to find those basic building blocks used for gaining mastery – the things that we have luckily not completely lost and has been recorded in books over the last two centuries. These skills aren't forgotten, they've just been shelved. *It's time to unshelve them once again and reclaim the lost knowledge of self-sufficiency.*

Based on this commitment to preserving our outdoors and handcraft heritage, we have taken great pride in publishing this book as a complete original work without any editorial changes or revisions. We hope it is worthy of both study and collection by handcrafters and outdoors folk in the modern era and to fulfill its status as a Legacy Edition by passing along to the libraries of future generations.

Unlike many other low-resolution photocopy reproductions of classic books that are common on the market, this Legacy Edition does not simply place poor photography of old texts on our pages and use error-prone optical scanning or computer-generated text. We want our work to speak for itself and reflect the quality demanded by our customers who spend their hard-earned money. With this in mind, each Legacy Edition book that has been chosen for publication is carefully remastered from original print books, *with the Doublebit Legacy Edition printed and laid out in the exact way that it was presented at its original publication.* Our Legacy Edition books are inspired by the original covers of first-edition texts, embracing the beauty that is in both the simplicity and sometimes ornate decoration of vintage and antique books. We want provide a beautiful, memorable experience that is as true to the original text as best as possible, but with the aid of modern technology to make as meaningful a reading experience as possible for books that are typically over a century old.

Because of its age and because it is presented in its original form, the book may contain misspellings, inking errors, and other print blemishes that were common for the age. However, these are exactly the things that we feel give the book its character, which we preserved in this Legacy Edition. During digitization, we did our best to ensure that each illustration in the text was clean and sharp with the least amount of loss from being copied and digitized as possible. Full-page plate illustrations are presented as they were found, often including the extra blank page that was often behind a plate and plate pagination. For the covers, we use the original cover design as our template to give the book its original feel. We are sure you'll appreciate the fine touches and attention to detail that your Legacy Edition has to offer.

For traditional handcrafters and outdoors enthusiasts who demand the best from their equipment, this Doublebit Press Legacy Edition reprint was made with you in mind. Both important and minor details have equally both been accounted for by our publishing staff, down to the cover, font, layout, and images. It is the goal of Doublebit Legacy Edition series to preserve America's handcrafting and outdoors heritage, but also be cherished as collectible pieces, worthy of collection in any person's library and that can be passed to future generations.

Every book selected to be in this series offers unique views and instruction on important skills, advice, tips, tidbits, anecdotes, stories, and experiences that will enrich the repertoire of any person looking to learn the skills it contains. To learn the most basic building blocks leads to mastery of all its aspects.

Studying This Book

The pages within this book present an overwhelming amount of information, facts, and directions to memorize that are often outdated and at the least, out of practice by modern standards. That doesn't mean that these pages have nothing to teach! It's just going to likely be new stuff for many readers.

Our one suggestion is *don't try to memorize everything,* especially when you're thumbing through the book or even reading it cover-to-cover. Many of our Legacy Edition books are antique or vintage. These writings from the late 1800's to early 1900's can be dense and out of style for someone not used to reading these types of books. Instead, gain some basic familiarity with each topic by thumbing through the pages, looking at the illustrations, and seeing the section headers. Then, choose a few topics or skills for deeper study.

Before you start a crafting project, or before camping or other outdoors trips can even begin, some planning and reflection is useful. First, it might be helpful to read through the book with plans in mind. The book can provide useful material for close study and reflection before you acquire equipment or head out to the field to practice.

Secondly, once you've come up with a practice plan, you will of course want to start doing tasks and skills. Doublebit Legacy Edition reprints all represent *learning by doing*, with each book containing many skills to master that have long sense been out of practice. But this is exactly why we print these books – these skills and methods should not be forgotten!

Any of the old artisans and tutors of woodcraft will tell you in their classic books that you can only truly learn how do stuff by *actually doing it*. Home study indeed does you well by using the many guidebooks that have been published over the previous 125 years. However, hundreds more lessons will become immediately available to you the moment you start with some of the old-style tasks.

For instance, before the days of camping outfitters, outdoors adventurers made their gear, which was tailored to their individual needs. Many experiments were done in the field to tweak their gear to get that ever-changing point of "perfect." Aside from experiencing wonderful lessons in history, getting outside and doing some of the activities this book will give you an appreciation for modern advances in outdoors and handcraft method and tools of the trade, as well as a deeper understanding of the foundations of outdoors and hand-craft life in the event that your gear fails you or you otherwise find yourself in situations where knowing the principles will get you unstuck fast.

If we were to tally up each of the individual tips in the Doublebit Library of Legacy Edition reprints, they would easily number in the thousands. The old masters represent centuries of previous knowledge that have been all but lost to 21st Century, technology-driven folks. To this point, although experience and *actually doing stuff* are the best forms of learning, taking a mindful approach to study of these works also benefit your development as a competent outdoorsperson and handcrafter.

You may also find it invaluable to take these volumes with you on your camping or other outdoors trips. In addition to having reading material on a variety of topics in the field for down time, you'll also find a thousand things to try in these pages if you're bored. Although skills may be best studied when in the field through experience and reflection, you may also study woods skills at home as well. Gaining familiarity through reading, videos, and other media are a great start toward building your ability toward gaining mastery in the field.

THE CAMP COOK

CAMP GRUB

AN OUT-OF-DOORS COOKING MANUAL

BY

ELON JESSUP

AUTHOR OF "SNOW AND ICE SPORTS," ETC.

NEW YORK
E. P. DUTTON & COMPANY
681 FIFTH AVENUE

Copyright, 1924
By E. P. Dutton & Company

All Rights Reserved

CONTENTS

CHAPTER		PAGE
I.	WELL-BALANCED CAMP DIET	1
II.	THE CAMPER'S GRUB LIST	12
III.	CONVENIENT CAMP FOODS	33
IV.	MEAT AND GAME	53
V.	MORE ABOUT FOODS	67
VI.	"PORK AND"	87
VII.	GO EASY WITH THE FRYING PAN	96
VIII.	TEA OR COFFEE?	107
IX.	KEEPING, CLEANING AND COOKING FISH	119
X.	COOKING WITH NATURE'S TOOLS	137
XI.	THE CAMPER'S DISH LIST	151
XII.	CAMP CRANES AND FIRES	168
XIII.	OUT-OF-DOORS FIREPLACES	183
XIV.	CAMP STOVES	198
XV.	CAMPFIRE BAKING	210
XVI.	FIRELESS COOKING	225
XVII.	KEEPING FOOD FRESH	238
XVIII.	PURE DRINKING WATER	248
XIX.	KEEPING YOUR CAMP CLEAN	263

LIST OF ILLUSTRATIONS

	PAGE
An Efficient Vest-Pocket Knife for Cleaning Trout	126
A Good All-Round Type of Knife for Scaly Fish	126
Path of Knife in Cleaning a Fish	127
Path of Knife in Skinning a Pike	129
Nesting Dish Outfit	161
Vacuum Food-Jar and Vacuum Bottle	166
A Single-Stick Crane	168
Crotched Stick for Single-Crane Support	170
Convenient Single Crane	171
Crane Arrangement for Holding a Number of Kettles	172
Pot-Hooks, Crotched Sticks and Wire	173
The "Split-Stick" Crane	175
An Effective Tripod Crane	177
Methods of Building a Simple Fireplace	185
Stone Fireplace Used by the Forest Service	187
Fireplace for a Permanent Camp	190
A Trench Fireplace	191
A Fire-Iron Having Folding Legs	194
Cast-Iron Box Stove	203
Two Types of Sheet Metal Stoves	203
Folding Gasoline Stove	205
An Oven Mounted on the Stove	207
Reflector Oven Before an Open Fire	211

viii List of Illustrations

	PAGE
Combination Semi-Open Type of Stove and Reflector Oven	216
Cast-Iron Dutch Oven	219
A "Featherweight" Model	219
Two Frying Pans and Two Baking Pans as Ovens	221
How to Make a Fireless Cooker	231
Side and Top Views of an Improvised Army Oven	234
An Improvised Hole-in-the-Ground Ice-Box	239
Construction of "Iceless Refrigerator"	243
Portable Ice-Box for Motor Campers	246
Boxing a Spring	259
Method of Attaching a Water Bag to a Car	261
Plan of Camp Fire and Incinerator	268
The Barrel Type of Incinerator	269
A Camp Kitchen Seepage Pit	272

ACKNOWLEDGMENTS

The author's acknowledgment and thanks are due to THE OUTING PUBLISHING Co. of New York, to *Field and Stream* of New York, to DOUBLEDAY, PAGE & Co. of Garden City, to THE BOSTON COOKING SCHOOL MAGAZINE Co. of Boston, to *Outers' Recreation* of Chicago, to ABERCROMBIE & FITCH Co. of New York, for permission to use material, either text or illustrative, in this book.

CAMP GRUB

Camp Grub

CHAPTER I

WELL-BALANCED CAMP DIET

RIGHT kinds of food, properly cooked, are as essential to life in the out-of-doors as they are to life in the city. The content of the camp larder is too commonly based upon the fallacy that camping develops a cast-iron stomach and that the food you eat doesn't matter so long as it can be transported comfortably and there is plenty of it. There is just enough truth in this belief to make the fallacy plausible.

Out-of-doors cooking is frequently called an art, but it is seldom referred to as a science. In contrast to this, modern indoor cooking is usually spoken of as a science. The two backgrounds are different. Yet in each case the human stomach is the same, and while its needs may vary to some extent with different modes of life, it must under all conditions be treated essentially from a scientific standpoint. That which the average camp larder needs is a little less art and a little more science.

Science, unfortunately, has a habit of becoming

a bit ponderous and involved, not to say contradictory, at times. Its methods of telling literal-minded human beings, such as you and I, how and what we should eat are no exceptions. Hence, sound basic needs are not always given the full attention which they deserve.

I am informed, for example, that the daily food supply which I, a man doing moderately active muscular work consumes, should furnish 3,500 calories of energy, 100 grams of protein, 0.68 gram of calcium, 1.32 grams of phosphorus, and 15 milligrams of iron. I am told to consult carefully a food-value list to make sure that I am buying and eating my food in the proper proportions.

This information is of very great value. Perhaps I really should, for the good of my health, frequently consult such a list. Maybe if I did, I'd live to be a hundred. Unfortunately, human nature being as it is, this system, so long as it remains couched in scientific terms, does not always prove workable. The camper is too busy to puzzle it out: one has to go fishing.

Being this camper, I do know, however, that when I am living upon a well-balanced, wide variety of wholesome food, I am arriving at practically the same result, thus automatically practising what the scientist preaches. And that is what I mean in great part by the advisability of paying some attention to the findings of science as regards the consumption of food. In case you have the time, inclination, and wish accuracy, figure the matter out in terms of science; lacking these, use your own good judgment.

One's own good judgment when allowed properly to function proves an extraordinarily effective agent. The eating of three meals a day for a period of one-third or half a lifetime is a foundation that should give the average person pretty fair standing as an amateur scientist on food matters. Uncomfortable experiences in this background have brought to light a varied array of scientific facts. For example, perhaps one has learned to one's sorrow that a steady diet of fried food is to be avoided, or perhaps again the digestion has suffered through lack of fruits and vegetables.

Curiously enough, there is a common tendency to forget all about lessons of this general nature when one goes camping. Doesn't it seem foolish to go to the woods for good health and come back with a stomach-ache? This does happen. But it needn't happen if one will only use ordinary common sense in the selection and preparation of food. And that is my chief plea.

There is a considerable amount of divergence between traditional pioneering ideas of diet and those of to-day. The older ideas are still practised to varying degrees in camping. To some extent this is inevitable. Some types of camping always will be essentially of a pioneering nature. Yet, the case of the present-day average camper is exceedingly well summarized by Horace Kephart when he remarks in the *Vacation Manual:*

Of course, the dyed-in-the-wool old-timer will deride all table luxuries as "knickknacks" and "bric-a-brac." His own notion of outfitting—bacon and beans, cornmeal and coffee—is a relic of the time gone by when the two B's and two C's were about all that could be carried into the untracked wilderness where camping was done.

But to-day, for one party that goes into such a country there are ten, maybe a hundred, who do their touring and camping in more accessible regions. And there is no speck of sense in these latter-day folk tormenting themselves with a dietary so meager and monotonous that they sicken of it before they are out three days. It is no sin against the Red Gods to treat your "tummy" as well in the woods as you do at home.

So far as the matter can be arranged when camping, we should live upon a diet which offers well-balanced variety of wholesome food. Modern science has taught us that good health demands this. Such a diet may consist of many different kinds of foods, but it is, none the less, a very definite thing. It is a diet which keeps the muscles strong, the blood clean, the body warm, gives energy, and offers successful resistance to low vigor and disease.

Well-Balanced Camp Diet 5

There are many individual foods which fulfill to varying degrees the first four of these requirements and some in addition the fifth. The right combination of several foods is essential, however, if we are to receive in the proper proportion all the elements of nourishment which we need. This is what we mean by a well-balanced diet.

Certain foods have exceptional capacity for keeping the muscles strong. Lean meat, fish, eggs, milk, cheese, dried beans, and nuts are the outstanding examples. Other foods are specialists in keeping the blood clean: vegetables and fruits are efficient agents. For warmth, we place a good deal of reliance upon fat meat (such as bacon and salt pork), butter, and chocolate. Foods which are especially valuable in supplying both heat and energy are sugar, bread, cereals, potatoes, and jam.

Low vigor and disease are resisted when we eat eggs, milk, and various kinds of cooked vegetables, especially the leafy varieties. Furthermore, science has recently been insistent that we supplement these with a certain proportion of raw fresh vegetables and fruits, such as onions, cabbage, grapefruit, lemons, lettuce, and tomatoes.

Thus, for example, a diet which is confined to meat, potatoes, bread, and cereals may impress one as being quite wholesome but in reality it is insufficient to meet body needs. The lack of additional essentials which are present in vegetables, fruits, and dairy products affects the whole process of nutrition.

In the city, most of us eat the proper food combinations by habit. We have the science of nutrition to thank for this. Gradually, during the course of many years, the right habits have become more or less crystallized. Everybody eats either meat or a meat substitute and vegetables. In addition, the orange or grapefruit that we have for breakfast and the salad at dinner is each an important element in health.

Science wholly approves and goes on to tell us that we should also eat each day at least one helping of cooked leafy vegetable and either nearly a quart of milk or its equivalent in dairy products. As a rule, we find upon checking up the amount of milk we pour upon cereals, the butter on the bread, the cheese with pie, and so on, that we have instinctively followed instructions. In other words, under normal conditions, the presence in the diet of certain proportions of carbohydrates, proteins, fats, minerals, and the mysterious vitamines are more or less automatic.

As regards people who live in the backwoods, the case is often times different. The tendency in this instance is toward a "lop-sided" diet. Difficulty in securing and transporting proper food supplies in out-of-the-way places is one reason for this. Lack of information concerning the bodily

Well-Balanced Camp Diet

needs of variety in diet is another. Atrocious cooking of the food is sometimes a third. The three together prove a health-shattering trio.

Certain types of mountain people who spend their lives far removed from town life serve as extreme examples of the fatal effect of a lop-sided diet. The heroic pictures which fiction writers paint of "sturdy" mountain folk are in some cases far removed from the reality.

I could take you for a day's walk far back in the Ramapo hills, for example, and show you numerous enlightening and dismal pictures of listless, health-shattered households, these living in the most health-giving of natural surroundings. Various charitable organizations have published many reports concerning the sickly condition of peoples of this sort. Lack in variation of food occupies a prominent part in all such reports.

The backwoodsman oftentimes has the insight to recognize the connection between cause and effect. The backwoods trapper or lone prospector not infrequently is a rule-of-thumb scientist of sorts. His mainstay may be salt pork and his cooking of it is perhaps a culinary crime, but he has the good sense to eat with it, foods that will keep away actual disease.

He would laugh to scorn a food expert who told him of the desirability of eating anything as fancy as a grapefruit or a salad, but he himself fills much the same need in another way. He is mighty glad to get hold of a few raw onions, a lemon, a cabbage, or a can of tomatoes, for he knows that these prevent scurvy.

It is the same way with ships that sail the seven seas. Some of these are known among sea-faring men as "lime-juicers" because the crew being forced to subsist mainly upon salt pork, scurvy must be held in check by a supply of limes. Even so, neither the trapper nor the sailor in such instances as I have mentioned can remain in truly good health while subsisting upon such a lop-sided diet. Malnutrition may be present amid plenty in case the plenty is not of quality and of the proper selection.

There is, as a matter of fact, more or less justification for the widespread consumption of fats and fat foods in out-of-doors life as indicated by the foregoing. Fat foods have higher fuel value than do any others; and the human furnace both demands and is capable of assimilating a greater amount of fuel of this variety when it is being worked hard (especially so in chilly weather) than at times when it is in a fairly sedentary condition. Thus, when an easy-going vacationist lives for a week or two upon the typical diet of a hard-working woodsman without doing the woodsman's work, he not infrequently pays a visit to the doctor upon his return to town. It is a case of too much fuel;

not sufficient attention to variety. The woodsman, as well, usually carries his fat-food fuel needs to extremes. The fault consists of consuming a surplus of one element of food at the expense of another.

This fault is a common tendency in camping, one which in some instances may be quite as applicable to nourishing foods as to those which are not especially nourishing. Rice, for example, is a favorite food and a very good food. It is possible to satisfy the hunger and supply the body with a large amount of nutriment by eating a meal which is composed solely of rice. Not infrequently this is done.

If, however, you were to climb a mountain after such a meal you might wish that you had eaten a little less rice and had supplemented this with foods which specialized in muscle building such as eggs, meat, or fish, or else perhaps more simple still, cooked either beans or cheese with rice. Energy is the long suit of rice and while it also contains a commendable proportion of strengthening elements, the latter need bolstering from other sources. Here again it is a mistake to consume a surplus of one element of food at the expense of another.

It would be folly to declare that a slight touch of this and a slight touch of that in the diet makes all the difference between good health and poor health. The diet as regarded as a whole is what is important. Too frequently in camp life it is lopsided when with some manner of forethought it might just as readily be a well-rounded whole. This does not mean a great variety of food at every meal, for such a menu is contrary to the simplicity which is always desirable in camp life; it applies rather to the day-to-day supply.

The average vacationist who goes camping and departs too radically from his home standard of a well-balanced variety of wholesome food is to varying degrees doing himself harm. He will find that when he exercises freely and the weather is cool his body demands a greater proportion of muscle-strengthening food than usual. And so it does in the city after he has played a round of golf or had a vigorous afternoon of tennis. But the body also demands vegetables and fruits in order to keep the blood clean.

The importance in camp life of good food, properly cooked, is indicated by Donald Hough when he says:

Grub is the most important part of the whole outfit and the first thing an outdoorsman should know well is its selection and preparation. . . . Food, of course, is not the object of such outdoor activities as canoeing, hunting, tramping, fishing, and the like; and a good meal is surely not the main end toward which a trip is taken; but I believe it to be the most important of those things which not only make the trip possible, but which insure the personal comfort and well-being of the camper, upon the success of which directly depends the success of the trip itself. . . .

The food, then, and how it is prepared is certainly the keystone upon which depends the success of any outing, and is therefore the most important item of all.

CHAPTER II

THE CAMPER'S GRUB LIST

A FAVORITE although puzzling indoor city sport as a preliminary to camping out is wrestling with the food provision list; the "grub" list it is commonly called. The grub list sometimes proves a formidable opponent, the reason being that such matters as personal taste and appetite, different kinds of camping, different ways of going, the time of the year, and the length of vacation periods are variable quantities that must be taken into consideration. Another point to be remembered is that you will probably be a lot hungrier when you get around to eating the food than you are at the time the list is compiled.

In all cases, our goal should be a well-balanced diet consisting of a reasonable amount of variety both in foods and cooking methods. As indicated in the preceding chapter, these foods must be a happy combination performing certain definite work. This combination should be of such a nature that the muscles are kept strong, the blood clean, the body warm, successful resistance is offered to low vigor, and the body acquires energy.

Such a goal is more readily available to some

The Camper's Grub List

campers than it is to others. For example, a diet that is wholly lacking in fresh foods is never a strictly normal diet. Yet, fresh foods become in some cases unavailable. One should, however, approach as closely to the goal as is practicable.

The food supplies of the camper who is always situated within easy access to food markets need not be noticeably different from that of the home supplies. A large army of motoring campers fall within this classification. A small ice-box attached to the car's running-board may serve as a means of keeping food fresh. A certain proportion of canned goods may be carried for the sake of convenience, but it must be remembered that a steady diet of canned foods is not good for the health. Many motorists go to extremes in this respect. I have seen cars that bore a striking resemblance to a traveling grocery store.

The camper who makes a prolonged stay in the wilderness, even though he has ample means of transporting plenty of food to his camp, is up against a different proposition. Fresh food is perishable and aside from fish which may be caught must largely be left out of the accounting.

It so happens, however, that fresh foods, such as dairy products and various kinds of uncooked vegetables and fruits, contain in their composition quantities of certain elements essential to health which most cooked foods possess only to a limited degree. These are the elusive vitamines which we have been hearing so much about during the last two or three years. So far as the average city table is concerned, the importance of the requisite amount of vitamines in the diet is now commonly recognized. Even as regards campers who tap freely fresh food markets, the vitamine needs usually automatically take care of themselves.

With people who are far removed from fresh-food supplies, the case is different. Backwoods campers do not as yet take vitamines very seriously. Their general attitude is perhaps well summarized by one old-time camper who remarks:

> The average camper's concern is whether he likes a thing or not and the practicability of getting it to camp, rather than the number of vitamines which it contains. What it lacks in vitamines he will make up in quantity.

A year or two ago I would have taken much this same attitude. In the meantime, however, I have been paying some manner of attention to the presence of fresh vegetables and fresh fruits in my camp diet. And I have come to the conclusion that while we cannot always get these in camp, yet, we cannot very well get along without them. Many old-timers will scorn the suggestion of a camp menu being decorated with a green salad, but I can assure you, it pays.

Scientific experiments have proved that the process of heating destroys some of the vitamine elements in food, but does not noticeably affect others. This is applicable both to canned food and fresh food that has been cooked. There seem to be certain exceptions to this destruction in the case of acid foods such as tomatoes and fruits. This is the reason why a can of tomatoes is oftentimes the saving grace in the limited diet of a backwoods trapper.

Average camp fare, even that of the old-timer who spurns the thought of vitamines, is in reality fairly prolific in two kinds of vitamines; these commonly known as Vitamine A and Vitamine B. It is the weakly member of the vitamine brotherhood, known as Vitamine C, the one which cannot stand very much heat that you need especially to plan for. In the city you receive this element largely in the form of uncooked fruits and salads, dishes which ordinarily are absent in camp fare. Although our mainstay must be cooked food, there is a small but important element which, for the most part, uncooked food supplies.

Have a salad of some sort in camp every day in case you can manage it. Such a dish becomes in some instances impracticable, but not always so. Cabbages when obtainable make good salads and onions are usually available. Take plenty of fresh vegetables and fresh fruits whenever you have at hand the facilities for buying and carrying these, or, lacking such facilities, take canned tomatoes, various other vegetables, and plenty of canned or dried fruits.

The elements of weight and bulk in food are with some campers of no great manner of importance while with others these are very important elements indeed. Numerous foods when either in their raw states or canned are composed largely of water. And water is heavy stuff to carry. Dried fruit serves as an example of the saving in weight and bulk by carrying a certain proportion of food from which the water is temporarily missing. More will be said upon this particular subject in the chapter which follows.

To come back to the bodily requirements as regards food in general: opinions differ concerning the specific foods and the quantities of each that constitute a well-balanced diet. The following rough summary compiled by food experts of the Metropolitan Life may serve as a helpful guide in a number of respects. This is called the "Day's Food." I will quote the suggestions in full:

A man of average size, who is moderately active, is likely to be well fed on a diet which includes the following:

One pound or a little less of bread or cereal food such as wheat, corn, hominy, rye, oatmeal, barley, buckwheat, or rice preparations.

The Camper's Grub List

Two ounces or four tablespoons of fat, such as butter, oleomargarine, corn oil, cottonseed oil, peanut oil, olive oil, meat drippings, etc.

Two to three ounces or four to six tablespoons of sugar, syrup, corn syrup, molasses, maple sugar or syrup, honey, etc.

About one-half pound of meat as purchased, poultry, fish, eggs, cheese, dried peas, beans, lentils, cowpeas, peanuts, etc.

One pint of milk. This may be in the form of a beverage or in milk dishes.

About one-third pound of potatoes or root vegetables.

About one-third pound fresh vegetables or greens or fresh fruit in season. If fresh fruit is too expensive dried fruits should be substituted.

The foregoing list, compiled for general utilization, does not coincide altogether with commonly accepted ideas regarding "hitting the trail" needs. For example, both the U. S. Army *garrison* ration and the Forest Service ration give an allotment of one pound and one quarter of fresh meat, whereas according to the foregoing, only one half pound is sufficient. The Army *travel* ration, on the other hand, gives only twelve ounces of meat, but increases slightly the bean allowance. Beans are a meat substitute, so this is largely a matter of convenience. The same sort of situation oftentimes arises in general camping.

Discrepancies, such as the foregoing, hinging

largely upon varying degrees of physical activity, are indicative of the difficulty of compiling the right sort of camp grub list. One-half pound of meat a day is probably an abundance for the vacationist who exerts himself but slightly, while on the other hand, one and one quarter pounds is none too much for the man who paddles a canoe all day or climbs mountains.

Horace Kephart, than whom there is no better authority on camp culinary matters, makes the statement that there can be no such thing as a standard camp ration. "Don't depend upon anybody's ration list"; he says, "do some figuring for yourself." Dr. Edward Breck, another excellent out-of-doors authority, says that published check-lists of rations are not of a great deal of value, persons and conditions varying too greatly.

It is unquestionably true that one must figure out the grub list for oneself. Bodily needs, as indicated in the present and foregoing chapter, are at once definite and variable. Human taste is variable; likewise, the form in which food is carried. The possibility of obtaining fresh fruit, vegetables, and fish in the section where one expects to camp is another consideration entering into the compilation of the grub list. It would be folly to load up with a pile of canned stuff in case the fresh articles were ready at hand. Of course, the catching of fish and killing of game is sometimes a gamble; due regard should be given to this element of chance.

Hence the value of planning your own grub list instead of accepting in whole the other fellow's. But the planning, to be satisfactory, must be done with some manner of system. L. J. Boughner offers, in the *Vacation Manual,* the following interesting suggestions as indicative of what is meant by system:

Take a large piece of paper and draw a line horizontally across the middle. Then divide it vertically by lines into compartments labeled "camp," "kitchen," "food," and so on. The top half is what you will take from home, the bottom half what you will buy near the camp. Make up a list now and keep it handy, for you will think of many additional articles from time to time.

When you are ready to start, use it as a checklist and when you get to camp, nail it up in the tent and amend it as you see fit. You will discard many things—take them to the bottom of the list under a column headed "Don't." Keep the list as long as you camp—it will always be useful because always changing.

Another element of wise planning is indicated by Wayne Northey in an article in *Outing.* The system used in this case is really the ration method, about which more will be said further on in the present chapter. Extracts from the article in question are as follows:

If the trip is for only a week or two, I usually figure about the amount of food required for one man for each day, then multiply that by the number in the party times the number of days the trip is to last. For example, let us say we want to know how much coffee will be required for four men for seven days. We know that a tablespoon will make two cups of coffee or enough for one man for one meal or three spoonfuls for a day. Thus, four men will need twelve spoonfuls of coffee for a day or eighty-four for seven days. . . .

By following this system it is possible to estimate in a short time the amount of sugar required for the coffee and so on down the line. In this way I go on through the twenty-one meals and draw up an imaginary menu until I get the total.

Of course, one should not become a slave to system. It should be used as a means rather than an end. Thus, the grub list should be planned with a view to offering various tasty cooking combinations in addition to the requisite amount of "straight" food. For example, when writing down on your list a staple camp food such as rice, bear in mind that a combination of cheese, rice, and gravy is such a wholesome main dish that it may take the place of meat. Or again, the presence of a few raisins gives you rice pudding.

It is the same way with many other foods. Cracker crumbs serve as a desirable touch to numerous dishes, flour may be used for making white sauce as well as bread, dried beef becomes a pleasing dish when creamed, macaroni is sometimes at a loss without cheese, dates go well in the breakfast cereal; combinations of this general sort should be planned for in the compilation of the grub list. These supply much of the variety that is essential to a well-balanced diet. This variety is of necessity more limited with some campers than with others. But even when transportation is an important consideration, a reasonably large amount of various kinds of foods need not prove a greater burden than few foods in large quantity.

In spite of the fact that a printed grub list can seldom be strictly adhered to in all particulars, it may, none the less, prove of some manner of value in the way of offering suggestions and serving as a working basis.

Suppose, for example, that two people are contemplating a two weeks' camping trip and that during this period they will be cut off entirely from all sources of food supply. This is hardly a usual situation these days, but it does not alter the fact that a list compiled upon such a basis may prove suggestive and be varied as conditions warrant. Two hungry active people should have plenty to eat and reasonable variety with the following provisions:

Fresh bread	4 loaves
Flour	10 pounds
Pancake flour	2 packages
Corn-meal	2 pounds
Baking powder	¼ pound
Soda crackers	2 small boxes
Pilot bread	½ pound
Cheese	1 pound
Eggs	2 dozen
Macaroni	1 package
Oatmeal	1 pound
Rice	2 pounds
Soups	3 small cans
Butter	3 pounds
Bacon	4 pounds
Ham	2 pounds
Salt pork	2 pounds
Corned beef	2 small cans
Dried beef	1 small can
Lard or substitute	1½ pounds
Canned milk	16 small cans
or	
Milk powder	2 pounds
Malted milk	1 bottle
Coffee	3 pounds
Tea	¼ pound
Sugar	5 pounds
Beans (dried)	2 pounds
or	
Canned baked beans	3 large cans
Split peas	½ pound

Lentils	½ pound
Raisins	1 package
Dates	1 package
Dried fruits	3 pounds
Canned fruits	2 cans
Fresh oranges	1 dozen
or	
Grapefruit	½ dozen
Lemons	½ dozen
Potatoes	15 pounds
Onions	3 pounds
Any fresh vegetables that can be kept fresh or	
Canned vegetables	8 cans
and	
Canned tomatoes	3 cans
Cocoa	½ pound
Sweet chocolate bars	1 pound
Nuts (shelled)	1 pound
Syrup	1 bottle
Peanut butter	1 small jar
Jam and jelly	2 jars
Salt	1 box
Pepper	small can
Mustard	small can
Salad dressing	1 bottle
Catsup	1 bottle
Canned fish	2 pounds
or	
Dried fish	1 pound

The foregoing list, as I have said, is compiled mainly by way of offering suggestions. Substitute and eliminate as your taste and needs dictate. If, for example, you have a grudge against salt pork (a perfectly reasonable grudge in warm weather), this food may be eliminated from the accounting. It is present mainly upon the chance that you will bake your own beans. Corn-meal is another cool-weather food that one should go light upon during warm days. Ordinarily, however, one should not skimp upon foods for which there is an almost universal out-of-doors craving. Prominent among these are butter, bacon, sweets, eggs, coffee or tea, and some breadstuffs. And if you are forced to forego fresh fruit, take plenty of canned tomatoes. In addition to their food value they are wonderful thirst quenchers.

Most of the foods included in this list are, comparatively speaking, imperishable. When fresh foods are available, liberal substitutions should be made in this respect. Fresh meat may be substituted for cured meat on the ratio of five pounds of fresh to two pounds of cured. In numerous instances the weight of the provision list as given must be kept down. This may be accomplished largely through substituting a certain amount of dried food. In the case of a hiking trip, a number of items must be eliminated entirely.

The most accurate and generally satisfactory method of figuring out a grub list is upon a ration basis. A ration is the amount of food considered necessary for one person for one day. Thus, by the process of multiplication the supply list may be expanded to suit any size of party or period of time.

Perhaps the best example of a ration list that aims toward great simplicity is the U. S. Army *travel* ration. This is designed for troops traveling otherwise than by marching and separated from ordinary cooking facilities. Because of lack of variety, it is applicable mainly to brief periods of travel. I give this ration list as it appears in an Army manual:

ARMY TRAVEL RATION

Component		Substitutive	
Articles	Quantities	Articles	Quantities
	Oz.		Oz.
Soft bread	18	Hard bread	16
Beef, corned	12	Hash, corned-beef	12
Beans, baked	4		
Tomatoes, canned	8		
Jam	1.4		
Coffee, roasted and ground	1.12		
Sugar	2.4		
Milk, evaporated, unsweetened	.5		

Probably the most suitable ration list that has been prepared for general camping purposes is that issued by the U. S. Forest Service as a guide in purchasing food supplies. This has been compiled with commendable care both as regards variety and proportions. It offers sufficient elasticity to permit one to pick and choose as one sees fit.

Probably one would not care strictly to adhere to this list throughout, but it offers many valuable suggestions that will prove quite worth while in the compilation of any grub list. The various weights of foods given are those of contents, exclusive of containers. The following list, on pages 27 to 30, is taken from a Forest Service bulletin.

On several occasions I have heard it declared that more good food is spoiled by poor cooking on a camping trip than under any other circumstances. Harold Pripps aptly remarks:

You can't enjoy the most entrancing view or even be decently sociable with your fellow men if your stomach is full of say—burnt beans.

Therefore, the need of some knowledge of cooking, concurrently with the compilation of a grub list and, in case this is lacking, the desirability of a certain amount of practise at home before going to the woods. Supplies are more easily transported from the corner store to the home kitchen than they are to the woods, and if mistakes are to be made, the former place is the more convenient place in which to make them. An open cook book

The Camper's Grub List

COMBINATION RATION LIST—ONE MAN ONE DAY

Balanced ration, one man, one day	Quantity	Weight in pounds	Equivalent substitutes	Quantity	Weight in pounds
Beef, fresh		1.25	Mutton or pork, fresh, or venison		1.25
			Bacon		.6
			Ham		.8
			Canned meat		1.0
			Canned fish		1.0
			Dried fish		.9
			Eggs	⅔ doz.	1.50
			Fowls or game birds, dressed		1.50
			Fresh fish, cleaned		2.0
			Cheese		.6
			Peanuts (with shells)		.7
Cheese		0.06	Meat, fresh		0.12
			Sweet chocolate		.06
Beans		.2	Dried peas, lentils, etc.		.2
			Rice or hominy		.2
			Baked beans, canned		.5
Flour		.8	Bread, baker's		1.0
			Pancake flour		.8
			Hard-tack or pilot bread		.7
			Crackers		.75
			Corn meal		.8
			Macaroni, spaghetti, etc.		.7

Camp Grub

COMBINATION RATION LIST—ONE MAN ONE DAY—*Continued*

Balanced ration, one man one day	Quantity	Weight in pounds	Equivalent substitutes	Quantity	Weight in pounds
Baking Powder	⅜ oz.	.048	Dry yeast (for yeast bread)	¼ cake	.012
			Soda (for sour dough)	2 oz.	.012
Oat meal		.15	Cream of wheat, corn meal, etc.		.17
			Grape nuts, corn flakes, etc.		.17
Potatoes, fresh		.8	Dried potatoes (evaporated)		.15
			Dried beans, lentils, peas, etc.		.2
			Rice or hominy		.2
Fresh vegetables (assorted) (onions, turnips, beets, cabbage, etc.)		.45	Canned peas or corn	¼ can	.31
			Canned tomatoes	¼ can	.47
			Dried or desiccated vegetables		.25
			Potatoes (added to staple allowance)		.40
			Dried apples		.15
			Raisins or currants		.15
			Dried peaches, figs, or apricots		.2
Prunes (dried)		.25	Canned fruit	⅓ can	.65
			Jam		.2
			Fresh fruit		.8
Coffee (ground, or soluble coffee)		.13	Tea	½ oz.	.03
			Chocolate or cocoa		.08
			Lemons	½ doz.	.65

The Camper's Grub List

COMBINATION RATION LIST—ONE MAN ONE DAY—*Continued*

Balanced ration, one man one day	Quantity	Weight in pounds	Equivalent substitutes	Quantity	Weight in pounds
Sugar (if no dried fruit is used, allowance may be reduced to 0.2 pound)		0.35			
Sirup[1]	1/12 pt.	.08	Molasses	1/12 pt.	0.07
			Honey		.08
			Sugar (white or brown)		.05
Milk (evaporated)	Can, ⅔ pt.	.33	Fresh milk	⅔ pt.	.66
			Condensed milk	1/6 pt.	.2
			Peanut butter		.13
Butter		.13	Oleomargarine		.13
Lard		.10	Lard substitutes		.10
			Bacon grease (can be saved if bacon is substituted for fresh meat)		.10
Salt	⅔ oz.	.04			
Pepper, black	1/17 oz.	.004	Red pepper	1/50 oz.	.0013
Pickles[1]	1/17 pt.	.05	Vinegar	1/32 pt.	.04
			Ginger	1/35 oz.	.003
Spices (cinnamon)[1]	1/35 oz.	.003	Nutmeg	1/35 oz.	.003
			Cloves	1/35 oz.	.003
			Mustard	1/35 oz.	.003

COMBINATION RATION LIST—ONE MAN ONE DAY—*Continued*

Balanced ration, one man one day	Quantity	Weight in pounds	Equivalent substitutes	Quantity	Weight in pounds
Flavoring extract (vanilla)[1]	0.03 oz.	.002	Lemon	0.03 oz.	.002
Cornstarch[1]		.2	Tapioca		.02
			Maggi soups	½ pkg.	.05
Bouillon cubes	0.1 oz.		Canned soups	½ can	.25
Total weight, 5.223.[2]					

[1] Suggestive rather than essential: their use may be governed largely by individual taste, size of party, and duration of trip.
[2] A much lighter ration can be made up by substituting the more concentrated foods within each class. As a rule, rations made up entirely of the most concentrated foods should be avoided.

Suggested accessories are soap, dish towels, hand towels, matches, candles, paper bags for lunches, and cloth bags for sugar, rice, beans, etc.

upon the kitchen table and a wife, mother, or sister within beck and call is a happy combination that is lacking in the woods.

Furthermore, there is almost invariably a turmoil, there are forgotten details and misunderstandings unless some one person shoulders the responsibilty for the grub list. Wayne Northey, after wide experience with various types of camping, carries this general idea further by saying:

Make some one responsible for feeding the gang. This will include getting up the grub list, preparing the supplies for transportation, care of the supplies in camp, and preparation and serving of the meals. I do not mean by this that one man must do all the work. He should merely be the mess sergeant.

There is no excuse for any one being idle during the preparation of a meal. Those who cannot cook (one cook for each meal is enough if he understands his business and has helpers) can do other work. There is always water to get and heat for dishwater, wood to be cut and piled for a rainy day, potatoes to be peeled, cans to be opened, and later, dishes to be washed. Anyone can do these jobs while the cook does the more important work of rolling biscuits, preparing mulligan, or perhaps trying to make something out of next to nothing for dessert. Do what you can. If there are two or more in camp who know how to cook, it is a good plan to change around with the work unless one is content to do all the cooking.

Proper timing of the cooking, a schedule that brings various foods of a meal to the table hot when they are needed is an important element that should be given due consideration by a prospective cook. Lacking this capacity for having the "food come out right," half of it is likely to be cold and soggy before its turn comes in the meal; or if you insist upon hot food, you may be forced to eat your dessert before the soup. Poor timing of this sort eliminates the sparkle from a meal. It is one of the greatest dampers on high spirits that can be found in camping.

This condition is obviated by the simple process of planning a meal before it is cooked; having the fire in the right condition, knowing the cooking times which certain foods require, and then being guided by this schedule.

CHAPTER III

CONVENIENT CAMP FOODS

THE size and weight of a package of food, imperishable qualities, and the convenience with which a given food may be prepared for the table are always important elements in camping, although with some types of camping these are of a greater amount of importance than with others. In all cases, however, we are more dependent upon various sorts of canned and dried foods in camp than in the home.

The fact that imperishable and readily transported foods have for many centuries been associated with camping trips in far-away places serves as some indication of their need. It is commonly and mistakenly supposed that dried foods are a modern invention. Yet, when the venturesome Marco Polo in the thirteenth century traveled through the heart of Asia, he found caravaning parties depending upon compressed dried fruits. There is not a great deal that is new in the world.

Modern science, during the past few years, has, of course, made big strides in perfecting these age-old ideas. The stock of imperishable provisions that the camping party of to-day takes to the woods is of a higher grade of quality and more palatable than a similar food supply of even ten years ago.

It is, to be sure, a rather ironic fact that as the goodness of dried and canned foods has increased, the need for these has to some extent, decreased. Fresh foods in connection with camping were, a few years ago, a rarity; the average camper of to-day, however, is likely to keep in pretty close touch with fresh-food markets. And fresh foods, when available, always are and probably always will be the best. Yet, at the same time, there almost always is the need in the camp larder for a certain amount of canned and dried food.

Convenient camp foods of this sort are seldom convenient in every respect. One must be guided largely by the particular variety of convenience that seems to fit best into one's plans. Thus, dried fruit has the advantage of being light in weight and small in bulk; very important elements as regards the camping hiker. But it also requires long soaking and stewing—certain drawbacks in case one is either in a hurry or lacks facilities for carrying an extra supply of stewed fruit.

Canned fruit, on the other hand, is altogether too heavy and bulky to be worthy of the hiker's consideration at all. Yet the camping motorist may find this weight no special inconvenience, while the fact that the can may be opened and its contents eaten immediately may prove most convenient. As against this advantage, there sometimes arises the problem of what to do with the uneaten portion of the contents. In this connection, dried fruit perhaps comes in for its innings, for in the case of dried fruit you have only to cook a sufficient amount for one meal. At the same time, small cans in preference to the larger sizes may prove a solution to the problem. One not infrequently finds it an advantage to take both dried and canned fruit.

The foregoing serves as an example of some of the elements to be taken into consideration as regards dried and canned foods in general. A lengthy discussion might readily be instituted upon the subject. Yet, in the end this would all simmer down to a question of personal needs, personal taste, and quality.

Quality is a very important element indeed, and this varies to a greater extent than many campers realize. Some canned goods are of high quality and most palatable while others are abominably poor. The same rule is applicable to various kinds of dried foods. Canned or package foodstuffs of poor quality possess slight food value and altogether are quite horrible. Get only the best.

The label encircling food which comes in the form either of a can or carton is usually a fairly accurate index to the worth of the content.

Granted the variety of food that one wants, most people know by experience the brands which may be relied upon. In case this experience is lacking, one may advisedly experiment first with small quantities instead of stocking up with an unknown article. The backwoods, far removed from supplies, is an inconvenient place in which to discover one's mistakes.

The label is not in all instances a safe criterion of the highest worth in food. There seem to be some foods which when treated by certain processes can never be an unqualified success, even with the best of intentions on the part of their manufacturers. Thus, there are a great many different varieties of canned meat, but only a few of these that one is likely to find especially palatable. More will be said about meat in the next chapter.

Canned fish is usually of a higher grade of quality than is canned meat. Fish, soups (some canned soups are delicious), vegetables, fruits, milk, various sweets, and other specialties are the fortes of canning. Yet, tasty as canned peaches are, I have eaten dehydrated peaches that I considered much better. On the other hand, I have never sampled any dehydrated pears that could equal canned pears. Personal taste, of course, may be largely responsible for such decisions, but this is, none the less, an important element.

I am critical of canned goods in general, yet, at

the same time, I rise in their defence. My criticism is aimed at their over-use. As I have indicated in the preceding chapter, this use is sometimes carried to extremes even when there is slight need for it. A diet that is confined to canned goods is far from being a normal diet.

I rise to the defence of canned goods upon two scores: first, that they are sometimes accused of being tasteless; and second, the danger of poisoning. Both of these possibilities may be obviated through wise selection and a reasonable amount of care. Lacking this selection and care, canned foods may in some instances prove both tasteless and dangerous. The following explicit instructions given by Horace Kephart in the *Vacation Manual* serves as an indication of what is meant by reasonable care. Mr. Kephart says:

The risk of poisoning could be reduced to practically nothing if users of preserved foods would exercise ordinary care in inspecting containers and their contents. A tin can of food should be flat or slightly drawn in at the ends, showing that no air has got into it. If swelled or bulged (except by being battered in transit) the chances are that the contents have spoiled.

If the food is in a glass jar, look for gas bubbles and note whether the product has become mushy or discolored. The lid should require some force to remove it, for the jar was sealed when the contents were boiling hot and this forms a partial vacuum which holds the lid firmly down so long as the seal remains perfect.

When the can or jar is opened, inspect the contents and discard any material that has an unusual appearance or odor.

Put the food to cook as soon as the container is opened and be sure it reaches the boiling point all the way through and keeps on boiling for a time. This is very essential.

There is no risk in eating acid vegetables (tomatoes), or fruits canned in syrup without heating so long as they have not soured. Acids and syrups prevent the formation of harmful bacteria.

Rust is to be regarded with suspicion. Good canned food keeps practically indefinitely (an obvious advantage in camping) so long as the cans are kept dry and reasonably cool. Dampness causes rust to form, which in time may result in tiny holes, thus spoiling the contents. Sometimes in country stores one is handed a rusted can that has reposed on the shelf for many long months. Hand it back and demand a shiny one in exchange.

It is inadvisable to allow canned foods to bask in a blazing mid-day sun. The reason for a fair amount of coolness surrounding the cans is that warmth increases any tendency toward attack of the food upon the tin. A more important chemical action to be guarded against is the very dangerous action which takes place when food is permitted to stand in an *opened* can.

Do not allow food to stand in an opened can. Pour it immediately into a dish. Of course, every one is familiar with a few possible exceptions to this important rule. One of these is evaporated milk; but even this will not keep in good condition for any great length of time. It should be used as soon as possible after being opened. For this reason, it is oftentimes a convenience to carry a number of small-sized cans of evaporated milk in preference to a few large cans.

Let us turn now to dried foods of various sorts. I use the term "dried" in its generic sense referring to several different processes. The common end in all cases is the reduction in weight from pounds to ounces without impairing the original qualities of the food and to make it imperishable. Results vary, but in great part are surprisingly successful.

From sixty to ninety per cent of the content of various fresh fruits and vegetables is water. Milk and eggs are both more than one-half water. As regards canned goods; the same general proportions hold true (with the exception of evaporated milk, which is a partially dried product). Furthermore, in the case of canned goods you have the additional weight in many instances of the syrup in the can and always that of the can itself.

Hence, the popularity in camping of dried foods such as powdered soups and powdered milk, dried vegetables and fruits, dried eggs and similar products. Most of these are partially cooked in the drying process although not thoroughly so as in the case of the greater number of canned foods. Powdered soup, for example, usually requires about fifteen minutes of boiling, dehydrated vegetables a little longer.

The most generally popular of powdered soups is an imported article known as "erbswurst," which originally was used as an emergency ration in the German army. Its content is a dried and ground mixture of pea-meal and pork. Sometimes known as "dynamite soup," it contains a very great amount of nutriment and for this reason is fine upon occasion, but should be used sparingly or else the diet will be lacking in requisite variety. Just why it came to be known as "dynamite" soup I do not know; some say because of its very filling nature, while others say because it comes in a package that has the general proportions of a stick of dynamite.

Various concentrated powdered soups made in this country are of the same general nature with the exception that most of these do not contain meat. Peas, beans, and lentils are some of the vegetables of which these are variously made—excellent and very nourishing foods. A three and one-half ounce package of this finely ground powder makes three pints of soup. And one bowl of

Convenient Camp Foods 41

it approaches close to being the main dish of a meal. Good canned soups of these varieties are fully as nourishing. But they represent more than three times greater carrying weight.

Beef extract is another form of concentrated soup which because of its convenience and supposedly nourishing qualities is used more or less in camping. Food experts seem agreed, however, that this is of slight value as a food although of some worth as a stimulant. It contains very little nutritive matter.

The choice between evaporated canned milk and powdered milk (which, to be sure, comes in a can) is largely a matter of personal taste. Both are most nourishing. Some campers remain devoted to the evaporated variety; in case they gauge the worth of all powdered milks by some of the first samples that were sold during the experimental stages of this new product, it is small wonder. I have tasted powdered milk that bore a striking resemblance to chalk. Manufacturers are now doing very much better. Two general varieties are sold, one being made from whole milk and the other from skimmed milk; always get the whole milk variety. Without doubt, powdered milk when mixed with water (about sixteen tablespoons to one quart of water) is more closely akin in taste to fresh milk than is evaporated milk.

It might be well to say at this point that my

statement early in the present chapter that fresh food is always the best when available, may be open to some qualification as regards milk. The milk situation is unusual. In a large city (such as New York) the milk which we drink has been sterilized before it reaches us; the law usually demands this. In other words, our milk is not raw; it has been cooked to some extent.

Similarly, evaporated and powdered milk have been sterilized. This makes them safe foods although perhaps not such agreeable foods as the sterilized milk which we drink in the city. Now, in the country the situation is usually different. Raw milk is commonly used. When you buy a quart of milk directly from a farmer, you get raw, unsterilized milk.

This tastes mighty well and the probability is that it will do you no harm. On the other hand, there is always the possibility that it contains unkilled bacteria that may do harm. Milk is animal food and any uncooked animal food holds this danger. Such milk may be pasteurized in camp and thereby become perfectly safe. Pasteurization consists of heating the milk to a given temperature for a certain period but never boiling it. The milk is then suddenly chilled. In case raw milk is used and there are small children in camp, this safeguard should always be taken. As regards adults, the matter is not of such great importance.

How she managed with three children under five years of age, far away from certified milk, is told by Hazel Langdale in a contribution to *Outing*. I will quote extracts from Mrs. Langdale's article:

We practically insured the children from the many stomach disorders so prevalent and so dangerous in the hot weather by pasteurizing the milk. This process ordinarily sounds so complicated that I am going to tell how we managed under camp conditions. It was really very simple.

The apparatus consisted of a large kettle deep enough to hold four quart bottles, a perforated pie plate, the four bottles, and a dairy thermometer. The milk was first strained through cheesecloth into the bottles, in one of which the thermometer was placed. The bottles, covered with paper tops, were set on the pie plate in the kettle and the kettle was filled with water and placed over the fire.

The water was then heated until the thermometer registered 145 degrees. For twenty minutes the milk was maintained at a temperature between 145 degrees and 167 degrees. The bottles were then removed and cooled rapidly by being placed first in cooler water, then on the ice. . . . I really believe that to this precaution we in large measure owed the fact that in all the time we were camping, the children did not have a single upset.

The foregoing refers, of course, to the raw product bought from the farmer. Mrs. Langdale's scheme is simple and practicable, but there is one detail which in my own experience I have not always found workable. An essential part of the pasteurization process is that the milk be suddenly chilled after the heating. But usually when I have tried this, the sudden shock of the cold has cracked and broken the bottle. I overcome this by pouring the hot milk from the bottle into an aluminum milk pan and placing this in turn in a larger pan holding cold water. To be sure, it is more sanitary to allow the milk to remain in the bottle and hence this is a better method if it can be made to work.

Fresh eggs being unavailable at times in camp, it may be well to depend upon egg powder as a substitute. This can hardly compare in goodness with the fresh article, but even so is preferable to whole eggs whose characters may be open to suspicion by the time you have cause to use them. Fresh eggs weigh about one and one-half pounds to the dozen; one pound of egg powder equals four dozen whole eggs. Powdered eggs are suitable only for scrambling and for cooking purposes.

Fresh eggs are more readily transported than is commonly supposed. The extensive manner in which eggs are shipped by parcel post serves as some indication of its practicability. The average camper should be able to do as well as the mails. A reasonable amount of care in packing is the main essential; a corrugated pasteboard box may be used as a container. When taking a hiking trip, I sometimes use an ordinary cardboard mailing-tube as an egg container, each egg wrapped in paper and a small wad between each two.

Dried fruits are of two general varieties. One of these is commonly referred to as "dried," while the other is known as a "dehydrated" product. The processes of manufacture are different. In the first instance, about twenty-five per cent of the natural water is permitted to remain in the fruit, while in the latter case practically all the water is extracted.

The dried variety is the one with which the greater number of people are familiar. For which reason, the following information concerning its use, contributed by a reader to *Outing,* is likely to prove of interest and value:

Now as to the preparation of the dried or more properly speaking "cured" fruits such as prunes, peaches, apples, etc. . . . I live and have my being not only in the Land of the Prune but in the very heart thereof, where the prune and the apricot reach the zenith of their pristine glory. Grower and packer know that more good fruit is spoiled before it reaches the palate because of ignorance in preparation than is dreamed of by most consumers.

Being engaged in the packing business, I talk by the cards. . . . I state most emphatically that cured fruits should not be "boiled until done," or at all, in camp or anywhere else. To do so spells ruination of the fruit for a table that values quality and flavor.

Prunes are virtually cooked all that is necessary before being shipped. . . Unless the prunes are opened and unduly exposed to the air for a considerable time, a Santa Clara prune is eatable from the box as a confection, or with a little warm water added, as a sauce. To make that sauce, pour some warm or tepid water on a quantity of prunes. Let stand for half an hour, wash, rinse, and drain.

Then put into the stewpan with the prunes enough water and a little more to allow for the prunes swelling to natural size; bring almost to a boil and put on the back of the stove to simmer or in a fireless cooker. Leave several hours to give the prunes a chance to take up the liquid. Don't put in any sugar unless unusual sweetness is desired. A good prune usually contains enough sugar for the average taste. Practically the same rules apply to apricots, peaches, etc. Pears need very little soaking.

Remember this: fruit in one form or another is an extremely important item in the camp grub list.

Manufacturers of dehydrated fruits and vegetables claim that their process gives one food which is a much closer approach to the fresh article both

Convenient Camp Foods 47

as regards taste and food value than is possible in the case of ordinary drying methods. In some instances I think that this claim is sound, although taken as a whole I have not noticed a great deal of difference between fruits that have been well dried and those that have been well dehydrated. It has been my experience that the choice of the brand is the main essential. In either case, some brands are very good while others are poor.

Lacking fresh vegetables or the facilities for carrying these, dehydrated vegetables fill an important need in camping. Canned goods are to some extent more convenient if weight is no object, for dehydrated products require an overnight soaking and then fairly lengthy cooking. Some people declare that dehydrated vegetables are more palatable than are canned stuffs. When the saving of weight and bulk is important, the dehydrated variety has the call.

In any case, do not slight the importance of vegetables in camp diet.

The following table compiled by one manufacturer of dehydrated fruits and vegetables is interesting in the light of showing comparative weights of various dehydrated foods as they are carried and those of fresh foods that would be needed to give the same amounts. The table is as follows:

DEHYDRATED FOODS:	Net Carton Weight	Number of Portions Each Carton Will Make	Weight of Fresh Product Needed to Give Equivalent of One Carton
FRUITS			
Apples	5 oz.	7 portions Sauce	3 lbs. 2 oz.
Apricots	5 oz.	6	2 lbs. 12 oz.
Cherries	4 oz.	4	1 lb. 14 oz.
Cranberries	2 oz.	6	1 lb. 1 oz.
Loganberries	4 oz.	6	1 lb. 6 oz.
Peaches	6 oz.	6	3 lbs.
Pears	5 oz.	8	2 lbs.
Prunes	16 oz.	8	3 lbs.
VEGETABLES			
Beans (Stringless)	3 oz.	6	1 lb. 14 oz.
Potatoes	6 oz.	6	2 lbs. 10 oz.
Soup Vegetables	1½ oz.	6-8	15 oz.
Squash	6 oz.	7	3 lbs. 6 oz.
Spinach	2½ oz.	6-8	2 lbs. 5½ oz.

The preservation of meats by means of dehydration does not appear to be very successful. Cured meats are more palatable. There is, however, a new process, distinct from curing, canning, and dehydration that does pretty well. The result is a small paper carton not much bigger than a postage stamp containing either dried roast beef hash or dried corned beef hash and weighing less than four ounces.

Only a few minutes of soaking are required for the contents, and these after being boiled for about twenty minutes (and then browned, if you like)

Convenient Camp Foods 49

offer a sufficient amount of food for two or three people. The notable convenience of this food commends it. To be sure, one would not care to depend upon it for steady diet. But a limited number of cartons are worthy of a place in the hiker's pack.

Canned fish, when used within reason, I consider one of the conspicuous examples of successful and convenient camp foods. Knowing the difficulty of keeping fresh and in eatable condition the fish which one catches oneself, I never cease to marvel at the results that are attained in this respect by modern canning methods.

Canned fish, because of its goodness and convenience, is used a great deal in camp life. Yet its outstanding drawback is equally applicable to almost any good food and this is: lack of variety either as to preparation or kind. Canned salmon is the best example of this fact. Salmon is a red-fleshed fish and therefore is unusually rich in fat. Hence, it fulfills a real bodily need among active out-of-door folk. There is good reason for the wide consumption of canned salmon in the Army.

At the same time, when you eat the same old salmon day after day served in the same old fashion, you soon get "fed up" on it. That, in varying degrees, is a common practise in camp life. If you wish to hear an expression of thorough distaste, ask a man who has been in the Army what he thinks of canned salmon. Which only goes to prove that you can get too much of a good thing.

Now a certain amount of variety in preparation makes a whole lot of difference. The simple process of heating the salmon offers a certain amount of attractive variety, while creaming, salmon loaf, and similar possibilities offer more. Creamed salmon is easy: merely make a white sauce of milk, butter and flour, and then after the skin and bones have been removed from the salmon allow the meat to simmer in this.

The foregoing sentiments are equally applicable to a number of varieties of other canned fish.

Dates, figs and shelled nuts are conveniently carried and highly nourishing foods. I invariably include nuts and either dates or figs in my own grub-sack. The latter two serve in great part as substitutes for the familiar prune. No criticism should be aimed at the prune, for it is a valuable food. Ordinarily, dates and figs take up no more room in an outfit and they give variety. George Fortiss offers the following suggestion which strikes me as being wise: taking into camp an allowance of one-half prunes and one-quarter each of dates and figs.

In speaking of nuts, Mr. Fortiss remarks that if you have a handful of shelled nuts and a cake of chocolate in your pocket and perchance you get caught out overnight, you will be a long way from starvation in the morning. The value of sweet chocolate in out-of-doors life is commonly recognized. A veteran camper will tell you that a cake is a concentrated meal. But the great nutritive value of nuts is too frequently overlooked.

Where to buy a certain kind of convenient camp food that strikes one's fancy is in some instances a problem. There is a stock expression that comes from the mouth of a groceryman when he hasn't got what you want, which runs as follows: "We used to carry that line, but there wasn't any call for it. We had to discontinue it."

For example, when in the West I developed a great liking for canned chili con carne (a plate of scrambled eggs surmounted by a can of hot chili con carne is a dish which once tried is repeated). In the West almost every grocery store has chili con carne, but in the East the only place that you can be sure to find it is a large store in the metropolis of a section.

Similarly, dehydrated foods, powdered soups, and other more or less unusual foods closely associated with camping cannot always be picked up on the spur of the moment either at the backwoods grocery store or the city corner grocery store. This is an element to be considered when a camp grub list is compiled. Hence, the desirability at times of getting in touch by mail with a large grocery firm in cities such as New York, Philadelphia, Boston or Chicago. Large camping outfitters in cities of this size also usually pay a considerable amount of attention to camp foods.

CHAPTER IV

MEAT AND GAME

FRESH, cured, and canned, are the three forms in which meats are ordinarily used in camping. The respective merits of these, taken as a whole, are in the order named. But even when fresh meat is readily available, the camp leader would be incomplete without a certain amount of cured meat, at least in the form of bacon; canned meat also may prove a convenience at times.

Under some circumstances, one's entire meat supply is of necessity confined to cured and canned products. Horace Kephart, speaking in general terms summarizes the situation very well when he remarks in the *Vacation Manual:*

Meat is the most difficult of foods to preserve without impairing its flavor. I have not found any canned roast beef, steak, chops, or the like that deserves the name. Boiled meat is better managed by the canners. . . . The various potted and devilled meats, intended merely for spreading on sandwiches are picnic stuff, not food for hardworking outdoorsmen. A jar of pickled lamb's tongue is nice for hot weather luncheons. . . . Cured meats, not canned, are the real stand-by of wilderness travelers—breakfast bacon especially.

Bacon, salt pork, ham, and dried beef are the four staple cured meats of camping. Of these, bacon is the familiar camp-fire classic and as a rule, the most important. Hardly any one would think of going camping without taking a supply of bacon. The Forest Service ration list given in Chapter II may be used as a guide in computing the amount that one needs; this shows that six-tenths of a pound of bacon is the equivalent of one pound and one quarter of fresh beef.

The form in which bacon is carried may be of some importance. For a camping trip of reasonably long duration, it is desirable that the bacon be kept in the form of strips and that you do your own slicing. Even during brief trips I like to carry my bacon in this form, although in this instance it is by no means essential. Boxes of ready-sliced bacon wrapped carefully in oiled paper are sometimes convenient for a few days' outing. Ready-sliced bacon that comes in jars is well protected against mold, but expensive.

Most bacon contains an insufficient amount of salt to prevent its becoming moldly after being kept for some time in a damp spot. Wipe off the mold and rub in salt.

Salt pork was the great food staple of the pioneer and still remains so to some extent. As Dr. Breck remarks, the opening of our great West by the explorer, trapper, and lumberman is under

Meat and Game 55

serious obligations to salt pork. Mr. Kephart, however, indicates the need for caution when he refers to salt pork as being commendable or accursed according to how it is used. Without doubt, the average camper should go easy as regards the consumption of salt pork. Bacon is a much safer food and serves equally well in most respects. An exception must be made, however, in the case of baked beans. A chunk of salt pork nesting within a pot of beans is very pleasing.

Smoked ham may give a good deal of pleasing "zip" to camp fare. One of its advantages is that it tastes well whether hot or cold. A point to bear in mind during the selection of a ham is, that the most tender variety of ham is the one which is encased in a layer of fat.

More important points to remember after you have it are that it must be kept well covered as a safeguard against flies and that it must be hung in a reasonably cool spot. Ordinarily, ham does not remain in good condition for a long time unless the weather is cool. In addition to the proverbial ham and eggs and bacon, ham combines well with various foods in the camp larder such as rice, onions, and macaroni.

Dried beef, in one form or another, has always been a staple food in out-of-the-way places, the world over. When reading of Arctic exploration, we usually learn that supplies of "pemmican" have been carried upon the expedition; this is one form of dried beef, something of a dry mince meat. The traditional "jerked" meat of the plains, meat that has been dried by the sun, is another form.

An interesting variation of this unsalted sun-dried beef is a home-cured product used freely in the ranch and mountain sections of South America known as "*tasajo.*" Sometimes the meat is cut into the form of a lariat and it is said that the natives occasionally find added usefulness for this in the form of a clothes-line. I recall reading of the astonishment of an American visitor upon seeing a native bite off one end of a clothes-line and toss it into a cooking pot.

Pemmican, jerked meat, and similar forms of dried beef are of slight value as regards average camping. Ordinary commercial dried beef, such as is sold by butcher or groceryman, is more practicable. This is not a food, however, to be taken into arid regions where good drinking water is scarce, for the eating of it keeps one insatiably thirsty.

I like to munch upon a slice of dried beef now and then while camping, but I find it at its best when creamed. This creaming process is very well described in an article in *Outing* by Margaret Hancock, which in part is as follows:

Some night when you are wondering what to have for supper, when fish is an old story and even

Meat and Game 57

bacon has lost its savor, put into your frying pan for each person to be served, a tablespoonful of butter, a well-heaped tablespoonful of flour, and an ounce or a trifle over of dried beef, separated into small pieces and with strings and fat removed. (This is about one good handful of the dried beef thus prepared for each two people.)

The mixture should be stirred over the fire until the meat gives off a savory odor and until the flour and butter are distinctly browned but not hopelessly burned. This will insure flavor for the resulting dish and keep the gravy from looking like an unwholesome flour-and-water paste. Even a little burning before the milk is added is preferable to adding the liquid before the proper browning is accomplished.

Then add a cupful or less at a time, either condensed milk diluted with water according to the taste of the company and the abundance of the reserve supply, or powdered milk thoroughly mixed with water, stirring constantly until you have a moderately thick, smooth gravy slightly brown in color and of appetizing smell. . . . When your gravy reaches the thickness and smoothness that you desire, you had better remove it from the fire until you are ready to use it and then quickly reheat it. Otherwise, it will become too thick and perhaps burn.

The uses of this gravy are various. Have you some wheat bread on hand that is getting a little bit stale? Toast it and without using any butter, pour over it some of your dried beef gravy. You will like the result. Have you potatoes, boiled or baked, dehydrated or fresh? You will find them improved by your creamed dried beef. Have you hot biscuit? . . . Hot biscuit with creamed dried beef are a delicacy indeed.

This is especially true if you are out on a long summer trip and your butter, in spite of precautions, is getting a little bit the worse for wear. Its shortcomings are particularly apparent on hot things, but the dried beef will successfully mask the defects of the butter used in the gravy and none other will be needed.

Any camper will find it to his advantage to re-read and remember the foregoing instructions as regards the making of gravy, irrespective of whether or not he uses dried beef in connection with it. Such a gravy, apart from its meat content, is of general usefulness in camp cooking. For example, creamed potatoes are made in the same general way, although in this instance the potatoes usually are not added until the gravy has thickened. Bacon grease may always be substituted for butter in case the butter supply is running low.

Canned meats, even though these are not always all that they might be in flavor, do, none the less, hold a distinct place in various phases of out-of-door life. The usefulness of potted meats for picnic purposes hardly requires comment. But the most satisfactory canned meat, regarded from the viewpoint of a real meal for a hungry camper, is perhaps corned beef.

Corned beef is not especially savory eaten cold, but when cooked with flavoring ingredients it becomes greatly improved. Various possibilities of this sort are worthy of being tried in case your meat supply is confined mainly to corned beef. For example, there is a cattle range dish of the Southwest sometimes known as "cowboy's delight."

This consists of two small onions and several potatoes boiling in a pint of water and a can of corned beef added when the potatoes are nearly cooked. Again, onions, boiled potatoes, and corned beef are mixed and fried in a pork-greased pan. Creaming is another method. Make a white sauce (according to gravy directions previously given) and turn diced corned beef into this. The dish is improved in case you then cover the top either with bread or cracker crumbs and place it in an oven to brown.

Scalloped corned beef is an additional possibility. The meat is chopped very fine. Remaining ingredients are bread crumbs, chopped onion, butter, chopped green peppers (if you can get them), and gravy. Alternate layers are made in the baking dish and then crumbs and gravy go on top. The Dutch oven performs excellent baking service.

It would be folly, of course, to place one's main dependence upon either cured or canned meat in case fresh meat were readily available. Camp methods of cooking fresh meats are fundamentally those of the home, although in some instances their exact forms may differ, as signified by primitive methods suggested in Chapter X, or the use of utensils such as the Dutch oven and reflector oven (Chapter XV).

In all cases, however, we have definite objects in view. Thus, as regards roasting and broiling, we wish to keep the juices within the meat in order to preserve flavor. This is accomplished through searing the meat on both sides by means of a great amount of heat; which seals the pores and prevents the escape of juices. After this preliminary searing, the meat may be allowed to cook more slowly.

Sometimes in camp we boil our meat. By plunging meat directly into a kettle of boiling water, the intense heat is a means of forming a desirable albuminous coating which prevents the escape of juices. Water which is below the boiling point permits these juices to escape. After the first vigorous boiling, however, the water may be allowed to simmer, for the coating on the meat is well set by this time and a lower temperature of the water does not perceptibly affect it.

There are times, however, when we really wish the juices from the meat to escape into the water. The result is the classic stew, a savory and whole-

Meat and Game 61

some dish. We intentionally enrich the water, the object being to have about half of the nutriment in the meat and half in the water. In this case, the meat is placed over the fire in cold water.

When vegetables are to be part of a meat stew, these should not be added until about a half hour before the cooking of the stew is finished. Up to this time the stew's activity has been slow simmering, but when the vegetables are added it should be boiling and continue to boil all the time these are cooking. Vegetables that are cooked below boiling point are likely to prove indigestible.

Experience is the best guide as regards the proper length of time that a certain meat should be cooked by a certain method. Conditions vary. Some fires are hotter than others, depending, for example, on how they are built and the kind of wood used. The following suggestions, intended for general utilization, may prove some manner of guidance.

A stew ordinarily takes between two and three hours. When so-called fireless cooking methods are used, it may be cooked all night.

The broiling of a beefsteak one inch thick takes from six to ten minutes; a one and one-half inch steak, about eight to fifteen minutes. The broiling of a lamb chop takes from six to ten minutes.

The roasting of well-done beef takes about fifteen minutes to the pound; if you like it rare, give it only ten minutes to the pound. In the same way, the roasting of well-done lamb takes twenty minutes to the pound; veal, twenty-five minutes; pork, thirty minutes; and chicken, fifteen minutes.

The cooking of game, because of its essentially out-of-doors nature, deserves special attention. By the term "game" I refer to hunted animals and birds. Fish are taken up in a separate chapter.

I might say there are some varieties of wild game commonly held in contempt as food which, if taken at the right time of the year and properly cooked, are really palatable. The following interesting extract from an article by Helen Campbell in the *Boston Cooking-School Magazine* concerning a French Canadian guide, tells its own story in a delightful manner:

And now Antoine went hastily to the spot, returning with the three-legged kettle from which proceeded an odor so delicious that the little party rose as one man to fall upon it.

"That is more like it, Antoine," they cried; and now they attacked the steaming platefuls he was serving, pausing with a smile of deep content as he watched them.

"You like it?" he said, as he offered the kettle for a second installment.

"Fine, Antoine! The best yet, and that is saying much; but I don't quite make it out. What is it?"

Meat and Game 63

"Dare I tell you, monsieur? I think so, now that you know it is excellent. It is what you cannot eat in spring when it is strong of its name, but now, yes; for it is autumn and no better meat can be.

"It is muskrat, monsieur. Pardon if I tell not in the beginning; for perhaps if I do, you never know it is a dish for epicures. . . . Ah, the hunter who knows has choice bits that he who buys in the cities never knows. They must be eaten in the woods."

The fretful porcupine is commonly regarded with the same disfavor as muskrat. Yet the first time I ate porcupine I was told by the camp cook that it was mutton and I believed him. It was most palatable. Porcupine meat, in common with that of such animals as muskrat, possum, and rabbit, is seldom fit to be eaten during the summer months. It is at its best in cool weather. Furthermore, a young porcupine or young rabbit is always very much more tender than an old one.

When game of this general sort is dressed, special care should be taken to remove every part that may add to its strong flavor. In the case of muskrat, only the back and hind legs should be saved. Parboiling after the dressing eliminates further undesirable features. It is usually advisable to parboil rabbit, muskrat, or porcupine, perhaps changing the water two or three times during the process. Certainly this should be done if the animal is to be eaten shortly after being killed. The meat after about fifteen minutes of boiling may be cooked in any one of various ways such as broiling, roasting, or stewing.

As a matter of fact, any kind of wild game whether it be porcupine, partridge, duck or deer, should be allowed to hang for some time between the killing and the cooking. Game that is cooked immediately after being killed is usually unhealthful, unpalatable, and tough. Deer is hardly in fit condition to be eaten until it has hung for a week. It takes that long for the carcass to become bled and thoroughly cooled. The same is true of moose and similar game. I became quite ill once from eating moose meat on the day following its killing. As regards most birds, of course, the hanging period need not be as long.

Immediately after an animal or bird has been killed, the entrails should be removed; the skin of the animal and feathers of the bird are allowed to remain. Then the game is hung in a cool, dry spot, care being taken to protect the meat from flies. A traditional hanging rule is "birds by the head, game by the legs." Some hunters, however, hang animals by the head, arguing that in this position they drain better. In case the game is to be kept a long time before being cooked, the inside should be rubbed with salt. A few pieces of charcoal may be added as a further preservative.

Meat and Game 65

Not infrequently it is impractical to allow game to hang as long as it should be hung. In one instance the weather may be dangerously warm while in another hungry campers may not be content to wait. Under such conditions, much of the strong, gamey taste and toughness may be overcome by resorting to the parboiling method which I have mentioned. Parboiling becomes impractical, however, in connection with some of the primitive bird-cooking methods that will be described in Chapter X.

There is an old saying which runs as follows: "Dress your duck and allow a slow cook to walk through a hot kitchen with it." The message which this cryptic saying seeks to convey is that a duck should be cooked fairly rare. Duck meat is dark and this in turn leads to a general rule as regards the cooking of game. This is: Game having white meat should be well cooked, while dark-meated game should always be rare.

There is a favorite way of cooking each kind of game. Roasting has the call in the case of venison and duck. The preparation of a venison roast is in all essentials similar to that of beef roast. The same comparison holds good in connection with venison steaks and beef steaks. The two main points of difference between the roasting of chicken and duck are the stuffing and the cooking time. Duck and all game birds, for that matter, are usually roasted without a stuffing, although there is no particular reason why one should not stuff them if one is so inclined. As regards the length of cooking, when a duck is placed in a hot oven it is likely to be done to the right turn in about a half hour. The meat becomes very dry in case it is overcooked. Red juice, not blood, following a cut of the knife is a safe criterion.

Young rabbit and squirrel are perhaps at their best when broiled, but the older ones should be stewed. Hence, the famous rabbit pot-pie dear to the heart of many a hunter, a stew made by long simmering of a cut-up rabbit and onions. Either biscuits or dumplings are usually added. A squirrel pot-pie is of the same general nature.

Partridge requires special care. Remember that its body is small and easily dried up. The bird should be turned frequently when being roasted. Slices of bacon are a profitable addition in that there is no fat in the meat.

The meat of practically all wild game is more highly flavored than that of domestic animals and fowl. This is a point to be born in mind in its cooking. The need for added seasoning is not so great.

CHAPTER V

MORE ABOUT FOODS

THE present chapter includes a somewhat random series of suggestions concerning various foods closely associated with camping, which elsewhere in this book receive inadequate attention—in a general way, the sort of thing that you file under the head of "Miscellaneous" in your letter cabinet.

Yet most of these foods are far from being unimportant. They deserve high rank in the camper's esteem. Prominent among these foods is rice, a most nutritious, easily digested, and inexpensive food that may to advantage be present in one's camp larder—and usually is present.

The weight and bulk of rice are not great. On this score its use is applicable to all classes of camping. The hiker as well as the motorist may with convenience carry a supply of rice. Some people, of course, do not like rice. Yet I wonder how many of these have given it a fair chance to prove its worth. Few foods, as a matter of fact, are as well suited to varied tastes. The mild flavor of rice is the reason; because of this it combines especially well with other foods, and thus one receives both flavor and desirable variety.

Adaptability is always a desirable quality in out-of-doors life, whether this take the form of mental attitude, dishes, or food. The outstanding virtue of rice in addition to its nutritive value is its adaptability. One day it becomes a breakfast cereal, the next day when combined either with meat or a meat substitute it is the main dish on the dinner table, at supper when mixed with almost any kind of fruit it becomes a dessert. And when the potato supply runs low, it serves as a worthy substitute for potatoes.

Much of the value of rice is dependent upon its being properly cooked. An old woodsman is credited with the remark that the water in which rice is boiled should be "not *jest* bilin', but bilin' like *hell*." Which, in a few terse words, sums up a considerable part of the secret of properly cooked rice. In other words, the rice grains must not be allowed to stick together and form a pasty mass.

Rice, before being cooked, should always receive a thorough preliminary washing through several waters in order to remove loose starch and foreign substances. One cup of rice, four or five quarts of boiling water, and one teaspoon of salt are about the right proportions for the most generally successful method of boiling rice. Pour the rice into the boiling water quite slowly. After about a half hour's boiling (due attention having been given to the old woodsman's advice) the water is drained off and the rice is placed at one side of the fire to steam for a short time.

The following comment by Donald Hough in *Outing* concerning another method of boiling rice (considerably less water being used in this case) is of interest:

It must be watched carefully as it nears the end of its cooking. Stir it, fondle it, coax it, take it off the fire, and put it back on for fleeting seconds, hold it so the fire will strike it on the side; and finally, just as it is right to the fraction of a second and the tension is at its height and the perspiration is running over your drawn face, thrust the bottom of the pail into the water—all to the end of getting as much of the moisture out of it as possible without burning it.

The following suggestion comes from George Stipp, likewise in *Outing:*

In regard to the use of rice, which is nearly all starch in composition, I would suggest that before starting on a trip a quantity be browned in the family oven as one would brown coffee. This turns some of the starch into a form of sugar and the rice will be found more healthful, at the same time palatable.

Corn-meal and oatmeal have always been used extensively in out-of-doors life, the main reason for this being that these both contain a greater amount of fat in their composition than do other grain foods. Fat gives the body warmth, and when we wake up in the mountains on a chilly morning we need some warmth. On the other hand, during hot summer days, warmth becomes far less desirable. Rice, lacking fat entirely, is in this case a more suitable cereal.

Corn-meal is the original American flour, and continues to be the backwoodsman's favorite. Its general usefulness commends it. Fish may be rolled in corn-meal before being fried; the attractiveness of a warm batch of johnny-cake hardly requires comment; or corn-meal is most palatable when eaten as a mush, the uneaten portions of which may be later fried. Corn-meal in the guise of mush requires at least an hour of boiling, and must be watched carefully near the end of this time or it will burn. In many instances it is advisable to mix white flour with corn-meal.

Food experts agree that the eating of any cereal food that is under-cooked does one more harm than good. The reason for this is that partially cooked starch and gluten are very indigestible. This is especially true as regards oatmeal. Properly cooked oatmeal has a great deal of value as a food, while, on the other hand, under-cooked oatmeal is quite indigestible.

Camp-cooked oatmeal, unfortunately, is too frequently of the latter variety, the reason for this being that a common camp practise consists of boiling the oatmeal as one would boil vegetables. The almost inevitable result is either a scorched product or one that is under-cooked.

It is practically impossible properly to cook oatmeal unless one makes use of a double-boiler or a fireless cooker. A crude double-boiler may be devised by placing one kettle within another.

Rolled oats (the variety of oatmeal that is commonly used), although partially cooked in its manufacture, requires ordinarily at least one-half hour of additional intense cooking. There are other partially cooked cereal preparations which do not require such long cooking and therefore simplify matters. These prove uncommonly convenient at times while camping, especially so during a hurried trip.

For example, I have in mind a palatable wheat preparation, which according to directions on its package requires only three minutes of boiling. There is no need for a double-boiler, and I have hot cereal in short order. Yet I always give this cereal at least five or six minutes of boiling. It is a pretty safe rule to double the time mentioned on the package when cooking any cereals of this sort.

Hot breakfast cereals are more generally popular in out-of-doors life than are the various types of thoroughly cooked cold products which may be poured directly from package to plate. During warm weather, of course, the latter have points in their favor, and their convenience at all times commends them. But most of these seem to lack the satisfying substance which is found in a dish of hot oatmeal. You notice this difference more in camp than you do in the city. Hot milk usually improves cold cereals.

Boiling food of any kind demands more attention than the average camper deems essential. Short-cuts may mean the sacrifice of flavor and nutriment. Cereals serve as one example of this fact. Vegetables are another.

In the boiling of any vegetable there comes a moment when this food is a happy combination of nutriment and flavor. Either before or after this moment, some element of palatability is lacking. As to just when the right moment arrives depends upon the age, size, and variety of the vegetable. Old vegetables have tough structures and hence demand longer boiling in order to break these down than do green stuffs.

In a list of a dozen different vegetables such as you buy in the market, you will find the proper boiling periods for these varying from twenty minutes to four hours; certainly a variance of sufficient width to warrant some attention. For example, an old beet cooked to the point of being

More About Foods

digestible requires from three to four hours of boiling. Some campers are so situated that they cannot wait that long; better none at all than under-cooked beets.

The following table may prove of value as an approximate guide to the proper boiling periods required by various vegetables. It is gauged from the time that the water begins to boil. As a rule, a vegetable should not be placed in the kettle until the water in the kettle is boiling. The table follows:

Potatoes	30 minutes
Corn	20 minutes
Beets (new)	20 to 40 minutes
Beets (old)	3 to 4 hours
Turnips (new)	30 to 60 minutes
Turnips (old)	2 to 3 hours
Cabbage	30 to 60 minutes
Onions	30 to 45 minutes
Spinach	20 to 30 minutes
Peas	20 to 30 minutes
String beans	30 to 40 minutes
Squash	1 hour
Carrots	30 minutes to 1 hour

In case you have ever camped in very high altitudes in mountainous regions, you have no doubt experienced the odd phenomena of having the water in the camp kettle boil surprisingly quickly, but take an uncommonly long time in cooking food. In high altitudes, all ordinary boiling time-tables run 'way off schedule as regards vegetables or any other food. For example, when you go high in the mountains, you must extend your three-minute boiling of eggs to five or six minutes.

The reason for this is that the higher we get above sea-level, the less the air pressure and the more quickly things burn. It must be remembered, however, that when under such conditions the boiling point of water happens to be, say, one hundred and ninety degrees, the heat of this water is not so great as that of the ordinary boiling point, two hundred and twelve degrees; which means that food that is boiled at an altitude of three or four thousand feet should be cooked for a longer period than in the case of lower altitudes. And the higher you go, the longer it must be cooked. This is a natural handicap. But it can be reduced to some extent if you cook with "soft" water. Most mountain water is "hard." Rain water, of course, is soft.

In Chapter III some mention has been made of milk. This very desirable food is deserving of further comment. Milk is sometimes called the "perfect" food. Its composition is perhaps a better proportioned mixture of the various elements that constitute a well-balanced diet than is to be found in any other single food.

Years ago, when I went camping in far-away places, we seldom carried a sufficient amount of milk with us. As a rule, we ran out of it before a trip was half completed; which was poor economy. That was in the days before the powdered variety had appeared upon the scene; to-day there is slight need for running short of this important food.

In case evaporated milk is used (which continues to be the favorite variety with many campers), a strip of adhesive tape pasted over the two small holes which you make in the top of the can is a fairly safe method of preventing the contents from spilling while in transit. I might add that adhesive tape is always a valuable adjunct to camping. Its varied usefulness ranges from binding a blister to mending a hole in the tent.

Butter is another valuable food that is better managed by the camper of to-day than of a few years ago. Hermetically sealed tins, together with a reasonable amount of care in keeping these cool, may delay the fatal day of rancid for weeks or even months. The more active a camper is, the greater the amount of butter he both demands and needs. "Please pass the salve" is a frequent request at the camp dining table. Which, translated into proper English, means butter.

I have before me a Department of Agriculture bulletin containing a graphic drawing which indicates both the merits and shortcomings of one pound of cheese. A series of formidable, very black lines show that this amount of cheese contains an astoundingly large proportion of certain food elements that are desirable to one's well being. Yet these elements are so very overreaching that I realize that if I were to eat one pound of cheese all at once, I would not be tempted to eat cheese again for some time to come.

Cheese is not usually given a prominent place in camp larders. As a matter of fact, it is a food that is peculiarly well adapted to camping needs. But it must be used with wisdom. It is a concentrated food and a comparatively small amount usually goes a long way.

Cheese, during the summer months, has the disadvantage of being liable to mold. It should be kept in a cool, dry place. A further precaution may be that of wrapping it in a cloth that has been dampened in vinegar. When either packing or keeping cheese, do not permit it to come into contact with other foods. Its taste is contagious, especially as regards butter. Cheese that comes in the form either of air-tight cartons or cans is oftentimes the most satisfactory sort for camping trips.

Camp bread calls for considerable comment. The universal necessity of bread is quite obvious.

The manner in which this need is met is dependent upon circumstances. The person who knows how to make home-made yeast bread and has at hand the facilities and time for doing so, may enjoy bread in its most nourishing and palatable form. The knack of making this mystic "raised" loaf is a gift that some people possess and others do not. The making of yeast bread in camp has three outstanding drawbacks: first, you cannot always get the yeast; second, the making of the bread takes time and is a good deal of a bother; third, the difficulty of keeping a constant temperature in the open.

Baking-powder bread, on the other hand, is quick and easy. Almost anyone can make it. And baking-powder bread, in one form or another, is the variety which is commonly used by campers who do their own baking. Unfortunately, a steady diet of this particular variety is not especially healthful.

So far as the average camper is concerned, the bread problem resolves itself into a question of how much baker's bread he can get and how much baking-powder bread he can stand. Baker's bread is generally available; almost every country store these days gets a fresh supply every day or two. The strict need for baking one's own bread has, to varying degrees, vanished in modern camp life.

This, however, does not alter the fact that some campers travel far back in the woods, others object to the carrying bulk of bread, while still others fancy the thought of baking their own bread.

The length of time that a supply of ready-baked bread which is taken from the city to the woods will remain fresh is largely dependent upon the condition of the weather. Warm weather is likely to mold and dry it up in a couple of days. With reasonably cool weather, however, it will remain fresh for an agreeably long time. The oiled paper in which most baker's bread is sold is, of course, a help. An additional protection that is advisable consists of carrying the loaves in an oilcloth-lined bag. Weather permitting, they should then remain fresh for a week or two.

Camp baking-powder bread and biscuits are identical, with the exception that the latter before being baked are fashioned into biscuit form. As Donald Hough aptly remarks, "the bread is biscuits." Sometimes it is more convenient to bake the biscuits in the form of a single loaf. There are a good many different ways of making baking-powder bread (or biscuits, if preferred), but in all cases it is a quick and convenient process, rarely taking more than a half hour from the time you pour out the flour till the completion of

More About Foods

baking. The following is a good recipe that makes ten small biscuits:

2 cups sifted flour
¾ teaspoon salt
2 teaspoons baking powder
2 tablespoons shortening
½ to ¾ cup liquid (milk, water or equal parts of each)

Flour, salt, and baking powder are sifted together and the shortening is cut up in this mixture with a knife. Liquid is added gradually and mixed. The dough is cut into the form of biscuits and baked about fifteen minutes, as a rule. The same recipe applies to "dropped" biscuits, although in this case the dough is made softer than in the foregoing. The dough is dropped on the baking tin by spoonfuls—hence the name.

The following recipe I learned from Howard Pulling, and have found it convenient upon occasion when taking overnight hikes, mixing the dry ingredients before leaving home and carrying these in a small bag:

> 1½ cups flour
> 1 teaspoon salt
> 1½ teaspoons baking powder
> 2 heaping teaspoons sugar
> About 1 cup water

Almost every amateur camp cook has his favorite baking-powder bread mixture. For example,

Donald Hough's is a proportion of two portions of white flour to one-half of graham to one-half of corn-meal, together with baking powder, salt, sugar, and liquid, and this, Mr. Hough optimistically declares, "will make anything from eclairs to brickbats."

There is another variety of bread intimately associated with out-of-doors life of which more or less frequent mention is made in stories and songs concerning the West and Alaska. This is "sour-dough" bread. In case you have ever lived on a western ranch, you have no doubt eaten this. It comes as a welcome relief after a steady diet of baking-powder bread, when one is far removed from supplies.

Sour-dough is in reality a variety of yeast bread in that it is made from a mixture that has been allowed to ferment. It is also essential that this mixture be permitted to turn sour. According to woods tradition, "the sourer the better." Hence the name. The fermentation and sourness comes from allowing a batter of the mixture to stand in a reasonably warm place over-night or longer. I recall hearing of a backwoodsman who made it a practice of sleeping on the mixture— that is, he dug a hole in the ground and placed the pail of batter in this.

The content of such a batter (mixed to medium thickness) may be warm water, flour, a spoon of sugar, and slight amount of salt—this for about one quart. Sometimes a touch of vinegar is added. After this batter has soured, most of it is mixed with more flour, a small amount of lard, and sugar and a spoon of baking *soda*. This is allowed to rise and then it is baked. Sour-dough has the obliging capacity for rising in almost any ordinary temperature. That part of the batter which is unused may serve as a foundation for the making of a new batch. This foundation hastens the desirable souring.

Corn bread is popular in camp. The following is a good recipe: ¾ cup corn-meal, 1 cup flour, ¼ cup sugar, 1½ tablespoons baking powder, ½ teaspoon salt, 1 cup milk, 2 tablespoons shortening. Dry ingredients are mixed and then the others are added and mixed. About twenty minutes of baking in a hot oven usually does the job.

Corn dodgers are easier; a convenient unleavened bread when some of the foregoing ingredients are unobtainable. Dodgers are made from a batter consisting merely of equal parts of corn-meal and water with a small amount of salt added. Some say the water should be cold and others say boiling. I am in favor of the latter. The mixture is baked in thin cakes in a frying pan, Dutch oven, or whatever oven facilities may be at hand. A hot stone answers fairly well in case these are lacking.

Many people like raisin bread. Raisins are included in most camp grub lists and some of these may readily be introduced into a batch of baking-powder bread. The following is a simple recipe: 3 cups flour, 1 teaspoon salt, 3 teaspoons baking powder, 1½ tablespoons sugar, 1½ cups milk, ½ package raisins, 2 tablespoons shortening. The addition of an egg, of course, helps.

In case any boiled corn-meal, oatmeal, or rice is left over from breakfast, it would mean a waste of good food to throw away such leavings. Each may become acceptable pancakes either at lunch or supper. The proverbial "mush" when fried and eaten with syrup is most attractive to the sweet tooth of a hungry camper. Or again, you can mix the cold mush into a flapjack batter.

At just what point bread ceases to be bread and becomes in turn the well-known camp flapjack is rather difficult to define. Various kinds of baking-powder breads are in reality baked flapjacks. Most flapjacks contain baking powder, the main difference being that the batter is thinner than in the case of bread. By the same token, an excessive amount of baking powder in the diet upsets one's stomach. One might just as well squarely face this fact as to believe that the alternate eating of these two attractive foods provides the desired variety.

I use the term "flapjack" in its general sense as

applied to various kinds of griddle cakes, although the camp griddle ordinarily is a frying pan. How you do beam with pride when you flip out of the pan a well-cooked flapjack coated by just the proper shade of brown! It is no mean accomplishment.

Having the pan neither luke-warm nor too hot is largely the secret, although the pan may be made very hot just before the batter is poured in. The formation of large bubbles *at once* on top of a cake means that the pan is too hot. In case the top of the cake becomes stiff before the under side is cooked, the griddle is not hot enough.

To turn a cake twice is an unforgivable breach of flapjack technique. When by gradual stages the uncooked top of a cake begins to bubble and then in turn becomes puffed full of bubbles and it is dry on its rim, the time has come to flip it.

Small packages of flour that are ready-prepared mixtures prove uncommonly convenient in flapjack making. But some campers will have none of these, declaring that the best flapjacks are those which you mix yourself. Here is a recipe for one kind: 1 cup corn-meal or oatmeal mush, 2 cups milk, 2 eggs, 2 teaspoons salt, 2 tablespoons sugar, 3 tablespoons shortening, $1\frac{1}{2}$ tablespoons baking powder. The following makes another kind of flapjack: 2 cups flour, 2 cups milk, 2 eggs, $\frac{1}{4}$ teaspoon salt, 3 teaspoons baking powder, and shortening. Or again, if you wish to eliminate the baking powder, try the following recipe: 2 cups flour, 2 cups sour milk, 2 eggs, ¼ teaspoon salt, 1 teaspoon baking soda, and shortening.

Sugar in one form or another plays an important part in out-of-doors life. The almost universal craving for sweets when people breathe fresh air and take exercise is too well known to require much comment. There are some outdoors goers who do not develop this craving but these are exceptions. Many times when in the woods I willingly would have given a dollar for a five-cent cake of sweet chocolate. Such a craving is not wholly a matter of taste. Sugar is a valuable energy-yielding food and the body demands it.

A person who exercises vigorously in the open can assimilate an unusual amount of sugar; the same amount if taken in the city would probably give him indigestion. Food experts declare that the amount of sugar that may be consumed without bad results is dependent largely upon the amount of exercise that is taken. Various types of camping with their relative degrees of activity fall within this category. It must be remembered that sugar in common with butter and cheese is a concentrated food.

Dried fruits, of course, contain a considerable amount of sugar. It is present as well in other dishes. Yet in addition to the sugar supply that comes in such form and for ordinary cooking and dining needs, the camper almost invariably is unusually grateful for the presence of sweets such as jam, marmalade, sweet chocolate bars, and either syrup or molasses. And don't forget the raisins. You will eat raisins when camping even though you have never liked them before.

A few words regarding food containers. Either for the protection of the food or convenience, sometimes both, it is necessary in numerous instances to carry food in other than their original containers. For example, flapjack flour, if left in its paper box, not only spills but it also becomes damp from the natural moisture of the woods. As a general rule, any food that is purchased in paper or cloth containers can to advantage be given a more protective covering.

The selection of such coverings is largely dependent upon the type of camping. Thus in motor camping or in a permanent camp it is usually possible to find good use for glass jars and friction-top cans. For hiking and canoe trips, water-proofed canvas bags are more feasible although even in these instances there are some articles such as butter, jam and coffee that had best be carried in the pry-up cans. Water-proofed food bags of this sort are sold by most outfitters.

Some foods as bought from the grocer are contained within oiled paper. This type of paper is a valuable safeguard against moisture and as a rule it should be allowed to remain. Indeed, an extra supply of oiled paper is a worthwhile adjunct to camping. It does well for covering meats, fish, cheese, and similar foods.

CHAPTER VI

"PORK AND"

SOME campers like their beans ready-baked for them, while there are others who prefer to bake their own.

Yet, they all take beans. The traditional "travel berry," as the common navy bean is aptly termed by woodsmen, occupies an important place in the camper's grub-sack, irrespective of whether he goes by motor car, by horse, or afoot. And rightly so, for beans are a nourishing, muscle-building food, a filling "main" dish that serves the hungry outdoors person as a worthy substitute for meat.

A given number of cans of baked beans, the familiar "pork and," goes down as one of the first items in the average camper's grub list. These beans have been cooked for you in the canning factory and with but a slight warming are ready to be eaten. They are quite as nourishing as are the raw, loose dried beans which one cooks oneself; certainly more so in case the loose beans are under-cooked. But whether or not the canned beans are as tasty is a point which is open to argument.

Any camper who has impatiently clicked his heels during the long, drawn-out process of cooking raw dried beans will bear witness to the great convenience, ordinarily, of beans that have been previously baked for him. Of course, when going afoot or taking a prolonged canoe trip, there are advantages in carrying a small package of uncooked beans in place of the more bulky, heavier cans. But there are other types of camping in which this is not so true.

In case your travels carry you to an altitude of much beyond four thousand feet, you may have your troubles in cooking raw loose beans, the reason for this being, the lowering of the boiling point of water at high altitudes. This drawback may be overcome to some extent by using "soft" water instead of the hard water which customarily is prevalent in mountainous sections. In other words, catch some rain water. As a matter of fact, beans always become less stubborn in soft water, irrespective of the altitude.

Whenever feasible, I like to include in my grub-sack both canned baked beans and a package of dry uncooked beans later to be baked in camp. For each of these varieties has notable points in its favor. Yet, as regards both, the full possibilities of the life-giving bean are not infrequently overlooked by campers.

Consider first, the instance of canned baked

"Pork And" 89

beans. These are commonly regarded and eaten as just plain pork and beans—no more, no less. Which is all very well upon occasion. But why not add sparkle to the camp menu now and then by varying the manner in which they are prepared for the table? As a matter of fact, a can of baked beans combines surprisingly well with a number of other food ingredients.

One example of this is the baked-bean loaf. Thus, in place always of eating your canned beans "straight," you may by way of variety, mash them, add a cup of crumbs, a chopped onion, an egg, half cup of milk, salt and pepper, make a loaf of this combination, bake it a few minutes—and there goes on the table an old friend in a new guise.

Another tasty baking combination is a tin of canned beans, a can of tomatoes, and a sliced onion. Various similar combinations may be readily devised.

Turn now, to the raw uncooked bean. How shall we cook it to the point of being both palatable and digestible? When under-cooked, it is neither of these.

Boiling is the quickest process; campers having limited time at their disposal cannot always wait for baking. The beans should receive a preliminary soaking in water lasting, preferably, several hours. Then they should be drained, placed in a kettle of fresh water, and boiled for about two hours. At the end of the first hour, either pork or bacon that has been parboiled is added to the beans. As the water boils low during the cooking process, more water, preferably boiling hot, should be added, although not very much.

After the beans are thoroughly cooked, you drain off the water, season them with pepper and salt, and then they are ready to be eaten. An agreeable finishing touch, however, is that of giving them a short browning in an oven. The reflector oven may perform able service in this respect.

The foregoing method is somewhat open to variation both as to cooking time and content. For example, you may, if you like, add potatoes or onions about a half hour before boiling operations are completed. But this method for the most part represents the shortest practicable time in which beans may be cooked without their becoming an insult to one's stomach.

To know beans at their best, however, to obtain the handsome dark brown color and the rich flavor that made Boston famous, we must really and truly bake them. And this, properly, is a process which from start to finish takes about twenty-four hours. The most convenient camp procedure in many instances consists of allowing the beans to soak in water all day, boiling them in the evening and permitting them to bake all night.

"Pork And"

The individual ingredients of a mess of baked beans vary to some extent with the supplies one happens to have at hand and the respective proportions of these vary, of course, with the amount of beans that are to be baked. Nearly every camp cook has his pet recipe for baking beans. The following has one quart of uncooked beans as its basis (which will probably last for a number of meals):

1 quart beans
½ pound salt pork
1 teaspoon mustard
¾ cup molasses (sugar, when no molasses)
1 teaspoon salt
Sprinkling of pepper
And possibly, a sliced onion

The method of procedure is as follows: Give the beans a long preliminary soaking, as previously indicated. Then in turn drain them, place them in a kettle of fresh water, permit this first to come to a boil, and then simmer slowly below the boiling point until the beans are reasonably soft. Which may mean anywhere from a half hour to an hour. As a means of knowing when to take the beans off, you may practise the traditional camp rite of blowing on one from time to time. When its skin splits open, the time has arrived to take the next step.

During the above-mentioned period that the beans have been parboiling, your chunk of salt pork should also have been parboiling in a separate utensil. Pork is now taken off the fire concurrently with beans and both are drained. The beans are placed in the bean bake-pot, ready at hand, and the pork, after being gashed with a knife three or four times, is buried in the center of the beans.

Various trimmings, as indicated in the foregoing list such as mustard and molasses, are mixed in a cup with boiling water, which in turn is poured over the beans. Additional hot water is added to cover the beans. The lid goes on the bake-pot and the beans are ready for baking.

The nature of the bake-pot and the manner in which it may be used is a subject demanding some comment. It may be an ordinary camp cooking kettle or a Dutch oven or a regulation bean pot either of iron or eathernware. Such a bean pot is desirable although not essential.

In case one's camp is supplied with a stove having a built-in oven, the bean pot may be placed in this and the beans baked at a *moderate* heat for about eight hours. They can be hurried along in a considerably shorter length of time, to be sure, but the long-drawn-out moderate heating process is the best.

In case one cooks with a camp fire, the bean pot may be hung over the fire. This, however, is usually too much of a hurry-up method to bring wholly satisfactory results. A better method consists of burying the pot in a mixture of hot coals and ashes. If an earthenware pot is used, do not allow it to come into contact with a flame, for this will crack it. Beans buried in the camp-fire ashes in the evening and left there over night will be ready to be eaten in the morning. And, as a rule, they are very good beans.

There is, however, another method of handling the bean pot which many old-time campers consider the best baking process of all. I refer to the traditional "bean hole." For example, every Maine logging camp has its bean hole. And if you have ever tasted a mess of these particular beans you will understand why their baking has not been instrusted to the convenient oven of the camp stove. Bean-hole cookery gives you beans at their best.

This hole-in-the-ground baking method consists of digging a hole about six inches deeper and six inches wider than the bean pot, building a hot fire in the hole and allowing it to burn for a half hour or more. This proceeding has the two-fold purpose of thoroughly drying and heating the hole and providing a bed of hot coals and ashes.

After this purpose has been attained, you rake out about half the coals and ashes from the bottom of the hole and lower the bean pot into the hole so that it rests upon those that remain. Fill in around the sides of the pot with coals and ashes, lay some upon its cover, and then fill the hole completely with dry warm earth or sand.

The cover of the bean pot should previously have been made tight as a safeguard against the entrance of dirt. Either a cheese-cloth washer or a paste-washer made from flour and water may serve. Then, with the beans buried completely under ground you may go to bed and forget all about them. They automatically attend to their own baking. Next morning, you haul the pot out of the hole, wedge off its cover, and before you is a mess of "beans as is beans."

This method of baking may be open to slight variations depending upon the construction of the hole and the nature of the bean pot. That which you wish is an even, lasting, subdued heat. Thus, in case a metal pot is used, it may sometimes be found advisable first to cover the pot with a layer of damp leaves held in place by burlap, before lowering it into the hole. This insures an even baking.

It is important in any case to dry thoroughly the earth before it receives the bean pot. For damp earth quickly dissipates all heat. The hole should preferably be dug within reasonable heating orbit of the campfire where the earth has become fairly well dried, rather than at some distance

"Pork And" 95

away. John Shegog remarks aptly in this connection:

To do first-class work you must have fine, dry sand, fine, dry gravel, or dry, friable earth. Whatever is used must be of loose texture and must be dry. To use wet material is almost an impossibility—or rather, is like getting the best of a lawyer, "possible, but not worth the work."

Rocks, of course, hold heat and sometimes one finds it an advantage to line one's bean hole with flat rocks before building the fire. Sand also holds heat and if you have this material available and dig your hole sufficiently close to the campfire there may be no need for using coals and ashes.

For example, if you have a campfire on the beach and plan for a bean hole, stir up the sand close by and around the fire so that the heat gets well down into it. Dig your hole in warmed sand, place some very hot sand in the bottom of this, then lower the bean pot into the hole and shovel a mound of hot sand over it.

The principle involved in this hole-in-the-ground method of cooking is that of the fireless cooker. Its application proves especially effective in the instance of baking beans, although it need not be confined to beans. It is also applicable to the cooking of cereals, stews, and similar dishes requiring long, even cooking instead of intense heat. Further discussion upon this fireless-cooker principle will be found in Chapter XVI.

CHAPTER VII

GO EASY WITH THE FRYING PAN

WHICH particular cooking utensil is it that you associate most closely with camping? The answer is simple. It is the frying pan, the romantic, temperamental camp frying pan, bolstered through generations by sentimental tradition—and responsible for more indigestion than any other article of cooking equipment that you can name.

Yet, of numerous camp cooking dishes which I possess, I am inclined to think that the one with which I would be most loath to part is a somewhat battered and distinctly blackened frying pan. Such is the power of a strange attachment which is a combination of tradition and pleasant memories and partly of actual need. And so it is with out-of-door folk the country over. In a camping trip of almost any nature, the frying pan is regarded as an indispensable piece of equipment.

The ever-capable frying pan is in many respects the most generally useful of conveniently carried utensils. In truth, it is a good half dozen utensils in one. You can bake, stew, or broil with it. And you can fry with it. Yes, there's the rub—you

Go Easy with the Frying Pan 97

can *fry* with it. In this particular capacity we find the frying pan's greatest strength and at the same time its most devastating weakness. It is with out-of-doors frying that the present chapter is largely concerned.

Frying implies the use of grease; and a steady diet of grease plays havoc with the digestion. This statement serves, I think, as a brief summary of the whole situation.

Kathrene Pinkerton has wisely remarked that a vacationist jumping from city ease to unaccustomed activity, whose suddenly augmented appetite greets any food as a friend, cannot but injure himself when he plasters his stomach with grease three times a day. This, unfortunately, is a fairly accurate picture of a large number of campers. These think and cook altogether too much in terms of the grease pot for their own good. And thereby they come to know the frying pan only at its worst. Dr. Edward Breck considers the frying pan "the greatest enemy of the woodsman."

The hungry camper, even though he be amply equipped with special facilities for baking, roasting, broiling, and boiling his food, appears to be insidiously fascinated by the thought of frying. A tender sirloin steak which his better judgment tells him should be broiled, potatoes and onions which he has planned to boil, all are sizzling in the grease-smattered skillet before he realizes the fact.

This action seems instinctive to the out-of-doors. Even the careful housekeeper turned camper often times approaches periously close to forming what has been aptly termed the "frying pan habit."

There are several wholly practical reasons for the widespread consumption of fried food in out-of-doors life, reasons which are essentially associated with camping; in city life these apply only to a limited extent. One of these is the element of speed. The out-of-doors appetite is more resentful of delay than is the city appetite.

The fisherman returns from stream to camp, wet and hungry, or the hiker from a long weary tramp through the hills. Each lights a warming fire, tosses open the camp larder, and reaches with right hand for the frying pan while the left settles firmly upon the convenient grease pot. Or again, a family makes camp in semidarkness at the end of a long day's motoring. There ensues a hurried rush to pitch the tent and start supper upon its sizzling way. An instinctive part of this rush is the act of reaching for the frying fat.

The grease-smothered frying pan is the quick and easy way. It combines the two-fold advantage of a quick lunch and a satisfying full meal. When not indulged in too frequently, the skillet in this guise may be justly regarded as a true and harmless friend. All good things, however, may be carried too far and the frying pan when made use

Go Easy with the Frying Pan 99

of repeatedly in such capacity is likely to prove a dangerous foe.

By no means do I advocate the elimination of the frying pan from the campfire. I hold only for wisdom and moderation in its use. The ancient Greek philosophy of "moderation in all things" is especially apt as applied to fried food.

A second reason for the great popularity of the camp frying pan and common over-indulgence in its use is that fried food tastes scrumptously good to an out-of-doors person. Here again, there is sound basis for the liking. Not only is it a matter of personal liking; actual body needs are also involved. A well-balanced diet contains in one form or another a certain proportion of fat. For fat supplies the body with heat and energy. It is not necessary, however, to satisfy this need with a constant diet of fried food, as is commonly the case. A great many ordinary foods that are cooked in other ways contain in their composition the requiste amount of fat.

Fresh air and out-of-doors exercise give one an especially strong craving for fats and, as I have indicated, this craving is usually satisfied in the form of the fat-soaked products of a skillet. Suppose, for example, that in the city you have a liking for boiled onions (which are very wholesome) but that later when camping you are asked to name the choice between onions boiled or fried.

You are likely to say "fried" (which are wonderfully tasty but not very wholesome).

Suppose, again, that in the city one is in the habit of having eggs which are boiled. Does one in camp spurn the inevitable fried eggs? Not that I have ever noticed. Various additional examples of this sort might be cited. The fault in each case is not so much in the fat itself as it is in the fact that food which is cooked in fat is at the same time likely to be greasy.

Certain types of backwoodsmen are extreme instances of the out-of-doors craving and satiation of fried foods. Backwoods cooking is sometimes atrocious. In Chapter I, I have indicated that lack of variation in diet is in great part the reason for this. Constant use and abuse of the frying pan plays an important part in this limited menu. Unvaried diet and constant dependence upon the frying pan proves a health-shattering combination.

The average camper seldom goes to the same extremes as does the backwoodsman in such matters. Yet, even so, consider the predominating presence of grease in what may be termed a by no means unusual camp breakfast. Flapjacks, eggs, bacon, and potatoes, we will say, all come out of the frying pan; fruit and coffee are the only items that escape it.

Some campers rise to this unvaried breakfast day in and day out. It tastes mighty good and with certain qualifications it is perhaps perfectly wholesome. These qualifications are, proper cooking and variety in method of cooking. You may allow the greased frying pan to predominate in this manner for one or two mornings a week without any harm being done, but why let it run away with one? Why not boil and poach your eggs now and then?

Or again, why always have your bacon fried? If you would know bacon at its best I suggest that you take it out of the frying pan and put it over the fire; broiled bacon is a very pleasant change. There is, to be sure, a certain element of truth in the suggestion of the old timber cruiser who said:

"You may as well fry her, for no matter what you do, she is only pork, after all."

At the same time, any one who has viewed the streams of grease which pour out of a piece of bacon is likely to admit that the broiling method is the more healthful of the two.

A good many out-of-doors people would hardly think themselves camping were the classic flapjack to be erased from the breakfast menu. And there is no reason why it should be erased, in case it is properly cooked. But why allow it literally to swim in grease as is so often done? The most tasty and wholesome flapjacks are those which bounce from a skillet which has been only slightly greased. I will quote some good advice upon this subject which Donald Hough gives in *Outing*:

> Poor flapjacks are the easiest to cook of any breakfast grub, and good ones the most difficult. ... Don't use too much grease. The frying pans may be thin and the fire hot, but there is no such thing as too small an amount of grease.
>
> More important still, if your cake sticks, do not pour grease around it to loosen it, for the grease will be soaked up as by a sponge; and in turning the cake, do not add grease to the pan merely because it looks dry. It may stick to the pan once in a while, but a little crispness is much better than a grease-soaked cake—ask your stomach.

At dinner and again at supper as well as in the case of breakfast, let the frying pan be used temperately and wisely whenever grease becomes an element in the cooking. The frying pan in itself is, of course, quite blameless; over-indulgence in the grease which is so closely associated with it is what plays havoc with one's digestion. As regards various camp dishes such as stews in which either water or milk take the place of frying fat, the skillet is quite above reproach.

Even when frying fat is used, the abuse of the frying pan is not wholly confined to its over-use. A surprisingly large amount of fried camp food becomes indigestable solely through being improperly fried. One element that is sometimes over-

Go Easy with the Frying Pan 103

looked in this connection is the selection of the food. As a general rule, the most suitable varieties of foods for frying are those which do not require a great amount of cooking.

For example, the frying of raw sliced potatoes as regards the ordinary facilities of camp life is seldom an unqualified success; the potatoes as a rule are not cooked through, the reason for this being that the frying pan alone gives an insufficient amount of cooking to soften the starch. The same holds true in the case of a number of other starchy vegetables, although there are, of course, various vegetables such as tomatoes and egg-plant, which may readily be fried in the raw state.

The most palatable frying result in the case of a starchy vegetable usually comes from starting it on its cooking way with a few minutes in boiling water, or in other words, by means of parboiling. This process softens the starch and then the frying pan may creditably finish the job. In much the same manner, left-over meats, cereals, and similar previously cooked foods are especially well adapted to frying. Various kinds of raw foods which do not require long cooking, such as fish, are also suitable.

The second important element in the proper cooking of fried food consists in permitting only the slightest possible amount of grease to permeate the food. This result is accomplished through allowing a layer of grease to form on the outside of the food while it is being cooked and later when ready to serve, taking care to drain off from the food as much of the clinging grease as will flow from it. An effective draining method sometimes used by campers is that of placing the hot fried food upon sheets of paper having absorbent qualities. This method, of course, is applicable only to fish, meat balls, potato balls, and similar dishes.

Any food that is permeated through and through with frying fat (in other words, "fat-soaking") is a calamity to one's stomach. Prevention of this condition is the first and last rule of healthful frying. And prevention is largely a matter of having the fat in the frying pan at a very high temperature before the cold food is placed into it. Thus, a layer of fat forms around the outside of the food, but does not penetrate it. On the other hand, food which is placed into luke-warm fat becomes fat-soaked through and through.

The heating of the fat must not be carried to extremes, for in such cases the exterior of the food becomes burned before it is cooked throughout. The fat in the pan is usually at the proper frying temperature when it begins to smoke. A time-honored test long used by housewives is as follows: When the fat begins to smoke, drop in a small piece of bread. It this turns brown within one

Go Easy with the Frying Pan 105

minute, the fat is considered sufficiently hot to receive the food.

A common mistake at this point, however, is that of placing too much food into the pan at one time, a proceeding which noticeably lowers the temperature of the fat and hence gives rise to a certain amount of fat-soaking. In case a number of small fish or meat balls, we will say, are to be fried, these should be placed into the pan gradually rather than all at once. Furthermore, the food should be as dry as possible, for the presence of water in it cools the fat. Fish, for example, should be wiped dry before being placed into the frying pan.

The use of a great quantity of fat in the frying pan does not necessarily indicate a less healthful result than does a small quantity of fat. As a matter of fact, when the cooking food is literally swimming in fat (deep fat frying), the result is likely to be the more healthful. The reason for this seeming contradiction is that in the case of deep fat frying, the fat may readily be brought to a high temperature, kept at that temperature, and the food being wholly immersed, the outside layer which quickly forms prevents fat-soaking.

With shallow fat frying on the other hand, only one side of the food at a time comes into contact with the hot fat, a condition which permits a certain amount of fat-soaking. As regards the ordinary facilities of average camping, however, the shallow fat frying method because of its general convenience is usually the more practicable of the two.

The way to prevent fat-soaking of the food when this method is used is to have the pan very hot before the fat is placed into it, using only a sufficient amount of fat to keep the food from sticking to the pan and having the fat in turn at the proper high temperature before adding the food. The frying of fish, vegetables, and similar foods demands a greater amount of fat than does the making of flapjacks.

In any case, the slightest application of fat that one can get along with short of burning the food is the proper amount. As regards the making of flapjacks, the rubbing of a bacon rind in the bottom of the hot pan is usually sufficient. But above all, never place the food in cold or luke-warm fat, for in this case the food thoroughly soaks up the fat. Which is the cardinal crime for which the romantic frying pan must be held responsible.

CHAPTER VIII

TEA OR COFFEE?

A CERTAIN story told of American troops stationed in England during the war concerns the British liking for tea. King George approached an American sergeant and affably inquired how he was getting along in England. British soldiers standing by, almost collapsed with horror when the American replied:

"Pretty well, King, but say, this tea we have for breakfast is fierce—can't you fix it up so we can have coffee?"

The sergeant got his coffee. But had he been buried with a North Woods guide in the wilderness of New Brunswick or Nova Scotia, a similar little comedy might have been enacted without the sergeant getting his coffee. For, tea occupies a more important place in the North Woods menu than is commonly believed. Not infrequently, it displaces coffee entirely.

The respective merit of coffee and tea as an out-of-doors drink is subject to perennial campfire discussion. An interesting debate concerning the worth of these two popular drinks appeared in *Outing* not long ago. M. A. Shaw started it by referring to tea as *the* drink of the open. Mr. Shaw says in part:

I once spent the night with two woods rangers in their shack in northern Ontario. They were in their second year of service and they told me that they drank only coffee when they came up first, but that gradually they had taken to tea and now drank nothing but that—clear. Trappers, hunters, and prospectors would, I believe, tell the same story.

It would be interesting to know why. For one thing, tea is convenient for carrying. It is light, much lighter than coffee and pound for pound goes much farther. A cup three times daily for one hundred days can be made from a single pound of tea. It is less liable to injury; for while both suffer from a wetting, tea will not under rough conditions deteriorate with age as coffee does. . . .

I myself am pretty sure that if I could take only one or the other of these two drinks into the woods, I should choose tea. All things considered, I prefer it.

Nor is it altogether a matter of agreeableness. I like coffee. Its odor and its taste are ravishingly pleasant. But I never found myself after coffee tackling the hard work of a cruise with the same vim and vigor as after tea. Long before I knew that it was the effect of tea, I have been fairly startled at a transformation in myself.

Time and time again, I have come to the noon spell, limp and lagging from a hard morning; and after a lunch with tea have taken again to paddling in such a manner as to discover with a kind of shock that I was keyed to a high pitch of vigor. No doubt of it, tea is for me more stimulating, more refreshing than coffee. But that's only a single instance, utterly impossible to generalize from—and there you are.

Richard S. Bond, upon finding his favorite drink, coffee, being assailed in the foregoing manner, took the matter so greatly to heart that he wrote to a number of prominent explorers and out-of-doors people asking their opinions as regards the relative merit of coffee and tea. These were published in a subsequent issue of *Outing*.

Dr. Wilfred T. Grenfell, to whom Labrador is an open book, replied:

Coffee is better than tea, as a temporary stimulant, in my opinion. Tea is more convenient to carry, unless some new production is forthcoming.

Dr. Robert F. Griggs, the Alaskan explorer, Director of the Katmai Expeditions of the National Geographic Society, gives the following as his experience:

We have, of course, tried both tea and coffee on our expeditions. In earlier years I always favored tea because of its ease of transportation. With the advent of soluble coffee, however, I began to experiment with it and found it very satisfactory. In 1917 we had a little of it and a good deal of tea. The coffee was exhausted in the first few weeks of the expedition; and some members told me that they, having the coffee habit, felt a decided deprivation which tea would not make good.

In 1919 we had both soluble coffee and tea in abundance. There were nineteen all told of us in the field, men of variable tastes and habits. Everyone used coffee freely, much more so than would be permissible to a man in sedentary occupations at home, but I do not recall having seen anyone make a single cup of tea. Of course, this does not answer the question whether tea might not have been better than coffee. It is simply an expression of the preference of that particular party.

The opinions of Vilhjalmar Stefansson, the famous Artic explorer, are in part as follows:

Men who engage in such work as mine soon get out of the habit of drinking either tea or coffee. It is too much bother. . . . The boiling of meat gives incidentally a broth which every man I have had so far with me comes eventually to prefer to either tea or coffee, no matter how fond he was of either originally.

With other Arctic explorers . . . tea or coffee have ordinarily been used. Whether such men prefer tea or coffee on the trail has usually depended upon which they preferred at home. The Norwegians, such as Sverdrup, tell us how refreshing coffee is; and the Americans, such as Peary, explain that tea is the only suitable drink.

The foregoing interesting array of opinions ranging from vacation camping to Arctic exploration would seem to indicate that by and large the choice between coffee and tea as regards life in the open rests almost solely with the individual. Coffee invariably occupies a prominent place in my own grub-sack, although not infrequently, a small package of tea resides in a niche beside it. For a quick "pick me up" in the middle of the day or the evening meal, tea is quite satisfying. But for breakfast—give me coffee.

This demand for my morning's cup of coffee instead of tea is purely a state of mind. I remember the first time I found myself with a guide in the North Woods and coffee entirely displaced by tea in the camp larder. The discovery came as a shock. Yet after the first morning of tea, the absence of coffee was not given another thought. For the tea filled the physical needs quite as ably.

The bulk and weight of coffee, so far as average camping is concerned, is no special drawback. Sometimes, however, the reverse is true. In which case, the soluble variety of coffee referred to Dr. Griggs has distinct advantages. About eighty-five per cent of the coffee berry consists of chaff, wood fiber, and similar by-products which may be eliminated without doing any special harm to the coffee.

Soluble coffee is coffee from which these by-products have been eliminated by means of a refining process. Thus, sixteen ounces of coffee berries are reduced to two ounces, upon the same general principle that an armful of sugar cane becomes through due process of refining, a pound of sugar. This soluble coffee dissolves quickly either in hot or cold water. Some people declare that it has not the rich flavor of ordinary newly ground bean coffee. And probably it hasn't. All will agree, however, that it proves uncommonly convenient at times in out-of-doors life.

Neither coffee nor tea contains any nutritive substance. Each may acquire a certain amount of food value through the addition of sugar and milk, but hardly enough to be of any special consequence. Basically, coffee and tea are stimulants —nothing more. Scientists say they are reasonably harmless stimulants for grown-up people when taken in moderation, although usually harmful to boys and girls.

Regarded from a strictly normal standpoint, it may be argued that a stimulant is seldom, if ever, necessary. Yet, the great value of stimulants in the form of tea or coffee as regards camp life is too obvious to require comment. There is distinctly more of a real need for these in camping, I should say, than in city life. Anyone who has rolled out of his blankets on a cold morning in the mountains or returned wet and fatigued from a fishing trip will bear witness to this.

To attribute to coffee and tea food value which they do not possess is a common mistake. Their

Tea or Coffee? 113

content in this respect is sometimes confused with that of cocoa, which has a considerable amount of food value. We must regard coffee and tea solely as stimulants. This means that the not unusual city breakfast which is confined to coffee and a slice of toast is pretty sparse nourishment. What actually happens is that the stimulant in the form of coffee depresses the hunger instead of satisfying it. Seemingly, one has had plenty to eat.

In sedentary city life, one may perhaps live on such a breakfast. But in the rigors of average camping it won't do. One needs quickly to institute a more nourishing program. Such a limited menu has no place in out-of-door life; one cannot live by coffee alone, as one soon discovers in the from of an "all-gone" feeling which appears about an hour or so following the camp breakfast that has consisted mainly of coffee. Remember this fact when you buy camping provisions.

On the other hand, one can, no doubt, drink more and stronger tea or coffee in the open without harm being done than would be possible in the city. Yet even in the out-of-doors there is need for moderation. The common tendency as regards camping is to use coffee and tea immoderately both in respect to quantity and strength. Through over-indulgence, a good thing is abused in much the same manner that the camp frying pan is commonly abused.

Every camp cook has his favorite method of making coffee, which he is by no means loath to admit is the only method capable of giving you the full flavor and aroma of the bean. After sampling many different results, I have come to the conclusion that the most important element in the making of good camp coffee is not so much the method as it is the man behind the method.

Perhaps the camp method which dictates that the coffee shall boil for three minutes cannot wholly be recommended. To have coffee actually boiling impairs its flavor to some extent and to allow it to boil for any length of time may do so seriously. It is also probably true that the process of mixing coffee with cold water and removing the pot from the fire immediately it boils up three times does, to a limited degree, impair the flavor. I have tasted mighty fine coffee made by the foregoing methods, but I consider there is a better way.

So far as ordinary camp facilities and ordinary ground coffee are concerned, I believe the best method to be that of bringing the water to a boil separately, placing the coffee in a dry pot and then pouring the boiled water over it. After which, the pot is placed in a moderate heat for about ten minutes while the coffee is allowed to steep. At no stage of the cooking does it actually boil.

The customary amount of ground coffee used in proportion to water is two heaping tablespoons to one pint of water. This proportion is sometimes open to a slight amount of variation, as indicated by the method of a timber cruiser with whom I once went camping in the West. His measurement system was more or less a matter of instinct. When I asked him how much coffee he used for a given amount of water, he drawled:

"I put in all my conscience allows and then add a little bit more."

I have found it convenient at times to buy coffee of the pulverized variety (not to be confused with soluble coffee). This is the ordinary bean which has been ground to much the same consistency as flour or powdered sugar. Then, before starting upon a trip, I have measured out a certain number of portions of this and confined each of these within a small muslin bag (the same idea as a tea bag).

At meal-time one of these bags is placed in the coffee pot and boiling water is poured over it in the manner described in the foregoing. Much the same result may be obtained by covering the top of the coffee pot with a square of muslin allowing its center to sag, placing the powdered coffee in this and then pouring the boiling water over it. In case the muslin is to be used again, it must first be thoroughly cleaned.

You can sometimes break supposedly infallible rules as regards the making of coffee and even then have a good cup of coffee. This, however, is hardly true of tea. For tea is either well made or poorly made. The two essential rules of tea making cannot be broken, these being: first, that the water must be boiling before the tea is added; and second, that it must *not* be permitted to continue to boil after the tea has been added.

Backwoodsmen in some sections have a custom of allowing their tea to boil. The result is a villainous concoction. Not content with this, they allow the leaves to stand all day in the pot, later add fresh water and boil again, thereby giving them a near-poison which is even more villainous and deadly than it was before.

Both in the case of coffee making and tea making it is important to have the utensils spotlessly clean. Absence of this care results in the absorption of undesirable ordors that detract notably from the flavor. Coffee grounds and tea leaves after being used once are ordinarily quite useless and should be thrown away.

One possible although perhaps unusual, exception to this is the purpose to which Siberian trappers put their exhausted tea leaves. They dry and save these and then when their boots get wet, place the leaves in the boots in order to dry these out. The tannin in the leaves readily absorbs the moisture.

Another possible exception is a South American

tea known as *maté*. In this case, tea may be brewed several times from the identical leaves that have been used before. Maté is not very well known in this country although in South America it is the customary drink of more than fifteen million people.

Maté has all the stimulating effects of coffee and ordinary tea, together with the further advantage of not keeping you awake at night. One's first meeting with this drink is hardly an unqualified success so far as liking goes, but in common with olives, it seems to improve with further acquaintance. Once in a while I take a small package camping with me in preference to ordinary tea.

There are two varieties of maté, one of these coarse and the other very fine. In using the coarse variety, the proper proportion is about one tablespoon to a cup and with the fine about one teaspoon to the cup. In either case you bring the water to a boil, place the maté in it, and continue boiling anywhere from three to ten minutes. Long boiling seems in no manner to detract from the taste.

Either the coffee or tea supply that one carries upon a camping trip should be kept in an air-tight and moisture-proof container. Both the bean and leaf soon lose strength and flavor in case they are exposed for any length of time to the inevitable moisture of the woods. Coffee which is carried in its whole bean state is, of course, in better condition to retain flavor than coffee that has previously been ground. The fact remains that ground coffee is the only practicable sort for average use in the open. This means that special care should be taken in keeping it well covered.

CHAPTER IX

KEEPING, CLEANING, AND COOKING FISH

DR. CHARLES STUART MOODY'S recipe for cooking trout is as follows: Rise from your downy couch while the stars are yet in the sky, don your wading boots, secure your creel, then tramp five miles over a steep mountain trail, hit the stream, and whip it back to within half a mile of camp. During that time you will have lain the foundation for the cooking.

Without doubt, the cooking of a fish which a camper catches begins long before it reaches the fire. There are three stages of preparation for eating. The first of these is the proper keeping of the fish between the catching and cooking, the second is its cleaning, and the third is its actual cooking. So, you see, the cooking of a fish really starts with the catching.

If you would eat your fish at its best, you must keep it in prime condition from the moment that it is hooked and landed. Care during this stage may mean the difference between flabby flesh and firm flesh. Properly to keep a fish means that it must be either wholly alive or wholly dead—never half alive, slowly smothering to death.

When you go lake fishing in a boat which is

equipped with a fish-well, you have the most practical means of keeping a live fish in sound condition. A good-sized mesh bag, or a floating wood box perforated with holes and floating at one side dangled from the side of the boat in the water performs the same service. In case there are no facilities of this nature at hand, the fish should be killed immediately after it is taken off the hook and should then be placed in a cool shaded spot.

That which keeps a dead fish right for cooking is the natural moisture of its body; this must be retained. Either too much or too little moisture is harmful to the flesh. The common practise of having a string of fish dangling over the side of a boat cannot be recommended. On the other hand, a freshly caught fish which remains in the sun for any length of time presently becomes unfit for eating. Fish deteriorate rapidly. And stale fish is poisonous. In Chapter IV, I have said that all wild game should be "hung" for a time before being cooked. This rule is *not* applicable to fish.

Some varieties of fish demand more care than do others. The best example of a fish demanding an exceptional amount of care is the delicate brook trout. Let us see how one of these speckled beauties may be kept in fresh condition. Dr. Moody aptly remarks that a trout properly prepared is "calculated to cause the gods on high Olympus to throw away their ambrosia in sheer disgust."

Keeping, Cleaning, Cooking Fish

When one follows a trout stream, one's only alternative after catching a fish is to kill it. With a small trout, a sharp rap on the head is usually sufficient, but there are some larger trout which die so hard that you may be obliged to disjoint the neck with your knife. The breaking of the neck by bending the head back sharply is another method.

If you plan to eat the freshly landed trout for supper, provided the weather is not extremely warm, you can postpone the cleaning of your catch until the end of the day. If you intend to keep your trout overnight or several days before eating, clean each immediately after it is caught. The trout is the most simple of all fresh water fish to clean; there is no scaling to be done, in the case of brook trout. You have only to learn the simple knack of making two quick cuts at the throat of the fish, slitting open the belly, detaching the gills from the top of the mouth, and then drawing out the entrails. Fins, tail and head may be left on.

In removing the entrails, however, be sure to leave undisturbed for the time being, a black streak of blood along the spine. This helps to keep the fish fresh. Eventually, it should be removed but not until the time when the fish is about to go on the fire. Either during or after cleaning, do not dip the trout in water. It is commonly held by knowing anglers that a trout should never be wholly immersed in water, once it has been taken out of the water by hook. Later it can be wiped with a dampened cloth, but that is quite another matter.

Whether you clean your trout immediately after they are released from the hook or delay the cleaning until later, a considerable amount of importance is attached to the care with which they are carried in the creel. Three points should be remembered in this connection: the trout must be kept cool, they must *not* be permitted directly to rub against each other, and they must be allowed to retain the right amount of moisture.

It is a common practise with anglers to line the creel either with moss or ferns and nest the newly caught trout within this cool soft bed. The next fish caught is laid in the creel in the same manner, care being taken that the two do not rub against each other. This is the method which I invariably use and I have always found it peculiarly effective in keeping the fish in prime condition.

There appeared in *Field and Stream* some time ago an interesting series of letters from readers offering various suggestions upon the subject of how to keep trout in good condition. I will quote in part from three of these letters. The first concerns the fern method to which I have just re-

Keeping, Cleaning, Cooking Fish 123

ferred. It is from P. D. Acers, and runs as follows:

The preservation of a mess of speckled beauties certainly is risky for any length of time, especially in hot weather or when they are transported from a cool altitude to a lower and warmer one.

On leaving camp I fill my creel full of fresh green ferns sprinkled with water. Ferns have in their composition cooling properties and keep trout cool and fresh for a long time. So as not to disfigure the fish I always see that my hands are wet before taking them from the hook; then, into the ferns they go. Before I get too many, if they are rising fast, I distribute them in my creel so that they do not touch, layers of ferns between.

At the first opportunity the fish are cleaned, taking out the gills, but leaving the heads attached. The gills seem to be subject to quicker decomposition than the rest of the fish. A few small ferns lengthwise where the entrails were removed helps also. . . .

On returning to camp, I place the fish in a fresh bundle of ferns and roll in a moist oilcloth. Plenty of ferns will do the trick for a delay of many hours, even in the sun. When I am home I remove the oilcloth and roll the fish in a moistened flour sack, or a piece of wet cloth; this tempers the freezing air from the ice just enough to keep the fish from getting stiff. I have kept trout for days with ice, but this letter refers to preserving the fish unfrozen so that they retain their original flavor.

The remaining two methods of keeping trout

I am not wholly familiar with from personal experience, but I give the letters because of their interest. One of these is from Harold H. Smedley, who says:

As soon after the trout are caught as is possible, I clean them and put them in my creel with moist leaves from fir trees. Upon my return to camp I have in readiness a large-mouth jar. This jar, for as long a time as is possible before being used, is placed in an ice-house, next to the ice, by cutting away the edges between two cakes or hollowing out one cake and covering it with sawdust which keeps it cold.

The fish are placed directly in the jar as soon as possible, it is re-capped airtight, placed back next to the ice and covered with sawdust. The jars should not be opened any more than is necessary after the placing of fish in it. . . . We are able to keep fish in this manner for almost a week.

The third letter is from Frank DeWitt Brown, who says in part:

In my own experience I have sat down to the table with a nice plate of trout in front of me and after one mouthful would wish the plate was a plate of fried eggs. To my mind, a trout should be in an absolutely fresh state. The finest mess of trout I had was last year and after keeping the fish a week, a friend to whom I gave some said, "Those trout were fresh caught." But I said, "No. They are a week old."

Here is the way I kept those fish: The weather

Keeping, Cleaning, Cooking Fish 125

was warm, in fact, hot, and the time was the latter part of June. As soon as I caught the trout I wrapped each fish in wax paper. For every fish I had a piece of muslin, about the size of a hand towel and wrapped each fish in the muslin. No two trout came in contact.

When I reached my hotel at night I wrapped the package of trout in a double thickness of newspaper and around the package I wrapped a piece of oilcloth. The package was then placed on ice in an ice-box. My catch the following day was prepared in the same manner and placed on ice. The important thing is to fold the muslin around each separate fish so that no two fish that are wrapped in wax paper come into contact.

On the second trip in July I did not follow the plan suggested, but instead bunched all the trout together and a muslin cloth around them. I lost all of them. There was no chance for the muslin to absorb the moisture as they were close in contact with each other.

So long as one keeps one's trout cool, separated from each other, and retaining the right amount of moisture, the method of doing so, perhaps, does not matter greatly. The foregoing suggestions, however, are indicative of the great care demanded of this most delicate of finnies if it is to become a palatable dish.

Scaly fish are not quite so susceptible to rapid deterioration as are trout in that their scales serve as some manner of protection. This protection, however, is not nearly so effective as it is generally believed to be. The same general principles of care are applicable. If you go lake fishing for pickerel or bass and have no facilities for properly keeping alive the newly caught fish, kill and wrap them in weeds or ferns. Sometimes it is

ABOVE: AN EFFICIENT VEST-POCKET KNIFE FOR CLEANING TROUT.
BELOW: A GOOD ALL-ROUND TYPE OF KNIFE FOR SCALY FISH.

advisable to clean the fish immediately they are caught.

The first process in the cleaning of the average fresh water fish consists ordinarily of scraping off the scales. Either a saw-tooth or blunt knife is a more effective weapon for this particular job than is a sharp knife. Lay the fish on its side, hold it firmly by the head and with a few swift sweeps with the knife, scrape the upper side free of scales. One finds with practise that the angle at which the knife is held is an element in the ease of scaling. The fish is then turned over and scaled on its other side.

Keeping, Cleaning, Cooking Fish 127

The next step demands a very sharp knife. You hold the fish firmly with one hand (I have found it wise upon occasion first to dip this hand in sand in order to give a firm grasp) and then with the knife in the other hand you make a fairly deep cut on each side of the back fin, running its length.

After these two incisions have been completed, you grasp the back end of the fin between the knife blade and the thumb and jerk it upward and forward. The whole fin comes out bodily and with it come rows of mean little spiney roots. This compete elimination of the back fin is a very much better method than the average fish-market man's practice merely of cutting off the fins with a pair of shears. For, in the latter case, the spiney roots remain in the flesh.

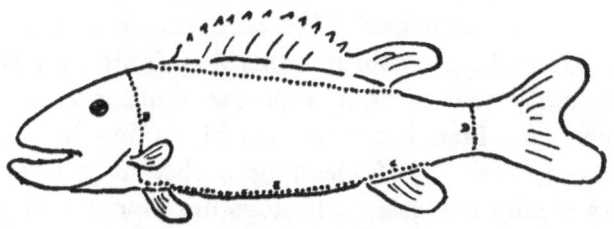

APPROXIMATE IDEA OF PATH OF KNIFE IN CLEANING A FISH. LETTERS INDICATE INDIVIDUAL INCISIONS AND CUTS MENTIONED IN TEXT.

Reverse the position of the fish in your hand so that the belly is now upward and proceed to eliminate the ventral fin (the one to the rear) in the same manner as the foregoing. The fish is now slit open along its belly and its head is taken off. The cut which takes off the head should slant toward the rear so that the side fins may come off with the head. The entrails are removed, the tail is cut off, the dark streaks of blood under the backbone are taken out, the fish is wiped both inside and out, first with a wet and then dry cloth, and it is ready for cooking.

The foregoing is, in a general way, the usual method of cleaning a scaly fish such as the perch, bass, or pickerel. It is open to more or less variety in specific instances both as regards the kind of fish and the manner in which it is to be cooked. In baking, for example, the head and tail are usually left on. Then, too, an angler is likely to develop with practise in fish cleaning, a certain individual technique. He becomes most efficient in eliminating waste motions and finds that surprisingly few strokes with the knife are necessary. In fact, after the dorsal fin has been removed, the act of cleaning a fish may become practically a single continuous movement with the knife.

There are some fish which prove better eating through having their skins removed, instead merely of being scaled. This is true almost universally of the bullhead and not infrequently it is true of perch, black bass, and pickerel in case these fish happen to live in murky, mossy, and fairly warm water. They absorb to some extent the imperfections of the water which they inhabit with the result that after being caught, cleaned in the ordinary manner, and cooked, they carry with them to the table a strong taste which many people find unpalatable. This taste, however, is mostly centered in the skin of the fish and through the elimination of the skin the taste is likely to go with it.

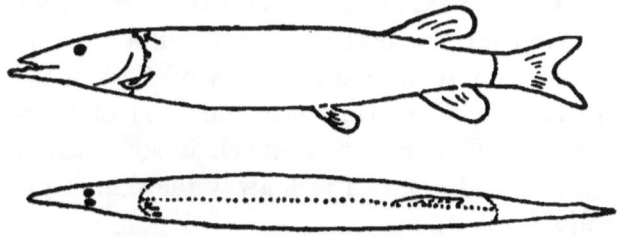

SIDE AND TOP VIEWS OF A PIKE, SHOWING PATH OF KNIFE PREPARATORY TO SKINNING. ARROW INDICATES WHERE YOU BEGIN.

Skinning a fish is a substitute for scaling. With a very sharp knife you slit the skin with a cut the shape of a half-moon on each side of the fish just behind the head. Circle the tail with another slit and then run the point of the knife the length of the fish's back. The incision along the back fin is made epecially deep and this fin is then removed in the manner previously described.

The skinning process consists of grasping with

the thumb and blade of the knife the loosened corner of skin above and behind the fish's eyes and with both a downward and outward pull, parting the skin from the flesh. After one side of the fish has been skinned in this manner, you return with thumb and knife to the nape of the neck and repeat the performance on the other side.

To skin a fish sounds easy and sometimes it is easy. Again, it proves a rather difficult task. Much depends both upon the fish and the person who does the skinning. There is a certain knack in taking off the skin so that it neither tears nor has clinging to it small chunks of flesh. In the case of fish of average size much as black bass, pickerel, and perch, this knack is soon acquired. You find that you can jerk away the skin in pretty handy fashion.

But with a big fish, such as an eighteen-pound pike, the situation is somewhat different. In this instance one needs to work slowly and with considerable caution; the blade of the knife under these particular conditions is in contact with the threads holding flesh and skin, although there is no actual attempt made to cut these. By way of analogy I might cite the example, gradually of opening a paper envelope that has been sealed by mistake.

If you find that the fish which you catch have a murky taste even after they had been skinned,

Keeping, Cleaning, Cooking Fish 131

try with your next string a liberal application of salt. After the fish have been cleaned, rub them both inside and outside with salt and then allow them to hang in a cool shaded spot for several hours. This treatment is almost certain to eliminate the taste. Fish such as the small-mouth bass, which make a point of inhabiting sparkling fresh water, seldom require either the skinning or salt treatment.

Knowing how to "bone" a fish sometimes proves an advantage. This knack as practised now and again in the North Woods consists merely of skinning the fish, slicing a thick strip of meat from each side, and then throwing the rest away. The cleaning of the fish is thus eliminated.

There is, of course, a certain amount of waste of good flesh in this way; furthermore, I think it advisable on general principles to clean the fish first. To "bone" a fish, you lay it on one side, after it has been cleaned, begin at the tail and run a sharp knife under the flesh close to the back bone, working toward the head. Then cut away the other side in the same manner. Fish that are especially prolific in bones prove difficult subjects so far as boning is concerned.

There is a rough-and-ready method of cooking an especially boney variety of fish such as the pickerel, which is a convenient combination of skinning, boning, boiling, and frying. Parboiling of the fish in salted water after it has been cleaned loosens the skin and flesh. This method is described as follows by Donald Hough in *Outing:*

Dump the fish into the pail of boiling water and let him boil for two or three minutes. Pour out the hot water and fill the pail with cold so that you can handle the fish. Then take each piece and remove the skin, which can be done either with the palm of the hand or the back of a knife. Separate the fish into the natural divisions of the flesh, removing the backbone and all other bones, which will come out very easily.

Roll the pieces in corn-meal and fry them. This manner of preparation may sound neither delicate nor appetizing; and certainly does not in any way coincide with the art of Mr. Walton, but I can assure all doubters that this way, aside from being quick, makes for a piece of fish which is "choicely good."

Camp methods of cooking fish fall, for the most part, into two classifications. One of these includes various primitive methods which are described with some detail in Chapter X. The other classification includes methods which are practically those of the home kitchen. The aggregate offers pleasing variety. I will comment briefly upon ordinary home methods.

Large fish, such as salmon, lake trout, and cod, are usually boiled. The water should be well

Keeping, Cleaning, Cooking Fish 133

salted; a small amount either of vinegar or lemon juice is of further advantage. It is advisable to wrap the fish in a piece of cheese-cloth, a precaution which prevents the fish from falling to pieces and also keeps off the scum. Thus the fish is lowered into boiling water. The complete boiling of a thick fish of the general varieties indicated requires from fifteen to twenty minutes to the pound. Don't boil a fish the good flavor of which is ruined through boiling. This is likely to prove true of black bass, while to boil a brook trout would amount almost to a sacrilege. Sea bass, however, are fine when boiled.

Medium-sized fish are usually best when broiled, baked, or fried. Certain qualifications must be made in regard to frying in that red-fleshed varieties such as salmon and lake trout are exceptionally rich in fat and therefore these are not especially well adapted to frying.

For broiling, large fish are cut in slices while smaller varieties are split through the back, although very small fish such as brook trout or smelts are broiled whole. Always grease the broiler so that the fish will not stick to it. And in releasing the cooked fish from the broiler, develop a technique which obviates the need of the fish traveling to plate in sections. Alternately loosening first one side of the fish and then the other usually proves successful.

The broiling time of a fish may range from five to twenty-five or thirty minutes, depending upon its size; a small brook trout may represent one extreme, a fair-sized pickerel or bass the other. A fish is sufficiently cooked when the flesh may be easily separated from the bone. This rule is applicable to any method of cooking fish.

The baking of a thick fish usually requires from ten to fifteen minutes to the pound; the baking of thin fish from eight to ten minutes to the pound. When this method of cooking is used, the head and tail of the fish are left on and the stomach is filled with a palatable stuffing and then sewed together. Lay a piece of cloth in the bottom of the pan so that the fish when cooked may be lifted out without falling to pieces. And perhaps cut two or three gashes on either side of the uncooked fish, laying upon these small slices of salt pork. Baked black bass filled with cracker crumb and onion stuffing—*there's* a lip-smacker for you!

Frying is the quick and easy way of cooking fish. Having the fat very hot before the fish are placed in the pan makes all the difference between goodness and ruination. The frying of ordinary-sized fish steaks usually takes from five to seven minutes; small fish fried whole such as brook trout from three to five minutes, although much depends upon the condition of the fire and the size of the trout.

Keeping, Cleaning, Cooking Fish

Dr. Moody emphatically declares that there are only two *right* ways to cook a trout. One of these is the primitive Indian method of holding the fish over an open fire on a stick. The other method is described with enticing flavor in an article contributed by Dr. Moody to *Outing*. I will quote in part:

Cut a thin strip of bacon and place it lengthwise in the belly cavity; sprinkle with pepper and salt. Your fish is now ready for the last rites.

If you have an old-fashioned Dutch oven in which to cook your trout you are thrice blest. If not, two heavy frying pans must be made to answer. Place the larger of these on the fire and heat it thoroughly, remove and smear with a bacon rind. Rake out a bed of coals, set the pan thereon, and place your trout in it. Take the smaller pan which has also been heated and invert it over the larger one, cover both with hot coals, and pronounce whatever incantation or burn whatever incense you choose for twenty-five minutes by the watch. I usually burn incense in the shape of a pipe of "dog leg" while my trout is cooking. Do not lift the cover while the work is progressing. Let it progress.

You might busy yourself in preparing a pot of coffee, a pan of potatoes, or whatever adjunct to the trout your fancy may suggest. At the expiration of the time, gently lift the cover and reveal a crisp brown skinful of white flaky meat, all the juices intact, all the aroma preserved.

If you happen to have a bottle of Worcestershire sauce or some such abomination, grasp it firmly by the neck, exert all your force and hurl it as far into the lake as possible. Good trout, like good wine, needs no bush.

CHAPTER X

COOKING WITH NATURE'S TOOLS

A FELLOW co-worker of the bubbling pot and sizzling pan declares that some of the supposedly simple backwoods methods of cooking fish and game without the aid of ordinary utensils are in reality "too darned fancy" to be of much value to the average camper.

To some extent, I agree with him. Few of these "simple" methods are quite so simple or so automatic as they seem. Perhaps the best example of this fact is the traditional woods custom of baking a fish in clay. Dr. Edward Breck indicates one difficulty when he remarks:

"First, find your clay; and there's the rub, for the proper stuff is very rare."

Although cooking methods of this general nature are the sort of thing which you make use of only upon occasion, they have, none the less, a distinct place in modern camping. Sometimes they prove a bit of a gamble, but the results when good are likely to be uncommonly good.

Popular backwoods methods of cooking fish without ordinary utensils range in variety from the baking of a good-sized black bass or pickerel in clay to the broiling of a trout on a sharpened green stick. I will describe first the traditional woods custom of baking a fish in clay.

Ordinarily, the fish is neither scaled nor cleaned. After it has been unhooked and killed, you gather several handfulls of soft clay and rub this all over the fish until it is completely encased in clay. In localities where clay is unavailable, mud is used, although this material does not answer so well.

The fish is placed for a short time in a moderate heat close by the fire in order to allow its clay coating to harden. Then it is nested within the much hotter heat of the embers. In a period varying from a half hour to two hours, depending upon the size of the fish and the intensity of the heat, you haul the clay package out of the fire and smash it open. The scales come off with the hard clay, the bones may be readily picked out, and the heat-shriveled intestines easily removed; leaving layers of firm well-baked flesh.

A more generally palatable clay baking method in some respects is that of cleaning the fish as you would for ordinary baking. That is, you split it open and remove the intestines but leave on the head and tail. Fill the stomach cavity with your favorite fish stuffing (which may be a mixture of bread or cracker crumbs, onion, salt, and pepper) and place thin slices of bacon or pork around the

Cooking with Nature's Tools 139

fish. Then wrap poplar leaves around the fish and encase the whole bundle in clay.

Gipsies, throughout the centuries have made a practise of wrapping food in layers of wet leaves and then burying it in the embers of an open fire. The leaves become charred from the heat, but the encased food cooks nicely and remains unscarred. Woodsmen make good use of this same principle in connection with the cooking of fish, although sometimes with slight variations.

The fish is cleaned, head and tail being left on, and then wrapped in several layers or large leaves which have been dipped in water. In the case of a large fish, a covering of paper is more practicable than are leaves; you wrap the fish in layers of paper, douse the package several times in water, and then bury it in the embers. Oiled paper is the best variety for the layer next to the fish, although newspapers do perfectly well for the remainder.

This method, when either leaves or papers are used, is a cooking process which is a combination of baking and steaming. Dr. Breck declares that a trout which is steam-baked in this manner is the last word in woods cookery. The cooking is not so much a matter of guess-work as in the case of clay baking, for the steam keeps the fish moist and this permits a certain amount of leeway. Furthermore, the fish may be jabbed with a fork or sliver now and then, as a guage of cooking progress.

Several variations of this method are possible. For example, Miles Bradford gives in *Outing*, the following instructions:

Take a sheet of old-fashioned brown paper and spread it thickly with butter, or, if butter is not any too plentiful, a mixture of butter and pork fat may be used. Wrap the fish in this; around the outside tie a goodly quantity of sprigs of sweet-fern and cover this again with three or four sheets of the brown paper.

Planked fish you have eaten in the city; and small need to call attention to the worth of this tasty method of preparation. But have you ever eaten it in the woods? Planking was not originated by a French chef, as some people believe. We have the North American Indian to thank for this commendable custom and it continues to be a favorite manner of cooking fish in the woods. Its outdoors application, however, is slightly different from that of the home kitchen; ordinarily, you stand the plank on end before the blaze of an open fire.

The preparation of a fish for planking is similar to that of preparing it for broiling on a wire broiler. That is, you split it down the back and open it wide. Next you fasten it wide open either to a flat board or a large piece of bark; slivers of wood may serve as tacks. The skin side of the fish is next to the board. Slices of bacon or pork are, as a rule, fastened to the upper part of the fish so that the drippings may flow down over it during the process of cooking, the idea being to give it flavor. The board is then propped on end before a rousing wood fire. When, in due course of events, a sliver can be thrust with ease into the thickest part of the fish, you will know by said token that the time has come to eat.

Bannister Merwin says that when he sees a mess of trout "brought to the table colored a dirty gray or in an unattractive coating of browned cornmeal" he feels as though an outrage had been done to nature. I give below Mr. Merwin's favorite method of cooking trout. It will interest you.

First catch your fish—but we have got by that point. Build your fire and let it burn until you have a good bed of hot stones and ashes. Have your trout, cleaned and washed, ready at hand on anything convenient. Pluck an armful of balsam twigs. Rake out your fire, leaving a base of hot stones and ashes. Upon this base lay balsam twigs till you have a layer from six to ten inches thick.

Now put your trout in a row upon this layer and cover with another layer of equal thickness; over all lay ashes and hot stones. Then smoke your pipe for say, twenty minutes or thereabouts.

When at last you gently remove the coverings, you will think at first that the trout have not been cooked at all. There they lie in all their moist beauty, colored as when they first came to your basket. But be careful how you handle them or they will fall apart, so tender are they. Steamed through and through by the heated essences of the balsam, they give out a faint aromatic redolence that adds a subtle perfection to the flavor.

Almost any trout fisherman will whole-heartedly advocate the pleasant outdoors custom of dangling a fish held by a green stick, over a glowing heap of hot wood coals. Yet, even in the case of so seemingly simple a process as this, the best results come only with method.

Try the following sometime: sharpen one end of a peeled green stick and thread this with a slice of bacon. Place the open fish lengthwise on the stick, enveloping the bacon. Sew up the stomach with a couple of sharpened twigs so that the fish will not fall off. Keep the fish turning slowly over the fire.

An important element in green-stick broiling, as regards fish or any other food, is the condition of the fire. That which we do *not* wish is smoked food. Although you can boil water over flames, you cannot broil properly in this manner. Only by hauling out the flaring chunks of wood or waiting until you have a hot bed of reasonably smokeless embers can you have properly broiled food. One reason why planked fish tastes so good is because of its freedom from smoke.

The clay-baking and stick-broiling methods described in the foregoing are equally applicable

Cooking with Nature's Tools 143

to the cooking of birds, even though the bird be nothing more game than a common barnyard hen. In the case of clay-baking a bird, it is customary to clean the bird first and then place a piece of pork or bacon within the stomach cavity. The feathers, however, are left on; these will later come off with the hardened baked clay. Jeannette Fox gives the following description in *Outing* of how a forest ranger prepared a sage hen for baking:

He lifted a bird as yet untouched by my hand and deftly cleaned but did not pick it. Then he sifted some dirt from the ground into a big mixing pan half filled with water. With these ingredients he mixed a paste of soft mud. Now he cut a slab of bacon which he placed inside of the hen with a good sprinkling of pepper and salt, at last stuffing feathers into the opening to keep the meat clean. This done, he covered the chicken with the mud paste.

Now he dug a hole deep enough to put the bird in. In the hole he built a fire and waited until there was a thick coating of coals on the sides and bottom. Next, he carefully placed the bird on these, throwing more coals on top. All this he covered with shovels of dirt until the hole was airtight. Now he turned to me and said, "It will be cooked in one hour from now."

At the end of the hour he came back again and throwing back the soil drew forth the chicken, quickly skinned it, and laid before us a delicately browned chicken with a wholesome odor about it.

The meat was more tender and juicy than a stove cooked one could be. A simple and perhaps more generally practicable method than the foregoing is that of enclosing a previously plucked bird in a flour and water paste and burying it in ashes.

To broil a bird on green sticks over an open fire necessitates, of course, its being plucked as well as cleaned. And to be cooked properly in this fashion it should be kept more or less constantly in movement, as in the case of fish which are broiled in the same general manner. A crotched stake at either side of the fire or two rocks may serve as supports for the horizontal stick which holds the bird.

The gipsies use a unique labor-saving device in this connection in the form of a row of green sticks planted in the ground at either side of the fire, their tops meeting directly above the fire and being held together by a piece of wire. The bird is suspended from this point by another length of wire and when given a good twist it rotates automatically, first one way and then the other. The natural springiness of the green sticks helps to keep it going.

Hot flat stones perform capable utensil service when ordinary cooking pans are lacking. A stone has an agreeable facility both for absorbing and radiating heat. If you build on top of a flat stone a blazing fire, allow the rock to become piping hot through and through, then sweep it clean of fire and ashes, you have a surface (in case it is the right kind of stone) upon which you can broil a steak or fry an egg. A pan covering the food, however, does no harm.

Cooking operations demanding a steadily hot, undiminished heat such as the making of flapjacks usually require that a fire be kept going under your flat stone utensil. In this case, the utensil may serve either as the top of a small stone fireplace or as a lid spanning two logs. Select a stone having a smooth surface and beware of those which explode or easily crack.

The clam-bake is an ancient and perennial example of the usefulness of hot stones. When we take a trip to the shore we are not happy until we have had a "bake." So, we build a steam table, or, in other words, an altar of flat rocks surmounted by a blazing fire. After the rocks have become thoroughly heated, we cover them with a foot layer of sea-weed, upon this place a bed of clams, perhaps a few ears of corn and maybe a bluefish wrapped in oiled paper, then another wet blanket of sea-weed, and perhaps over all an old sail cloth. A combined steaming and baking process somewhat similar to the previously described leaves—baked fish is the result.

Some day you may have cause to make use of the method by which the Indian cooked his stews.

In doing so, you choose either a small hollow stump or a rock having a convenient pot-hole and in this hole place the cold stew. Meantime, you have heating in a fire close by, a number of small stones. When these stones have become extremely hot you drop them, one after another into the stew. Water, of course, may be warmed by the same process.

Strictly speaking, there are no modern cooking and dining utensils which are essential to out-of-doors cooking. We would, in case we either were forced or wished to do so, enter the woods empty-handed so far as utensils were concerned and we could in crude fashion duplicate almost any kind of plain cooking that is practised on the kitchen range.

But, how, one well may inquire, can one boil water without having a metal bucket? Visit, some day, the Indian exhibit in the American Museum of Natural History, New York; note the native resourcefulness of the Indian as regards the construction of birch-bark utensils and in this resourcefulness you will have the correct answer. The Indian made a birch-bark bucket in which to boil water.

So far as the average out-of-doors person of today is concerned, such a device may be classified as a "stunt," having slight practical value. Still, it is an interesting thing to know about. Everything that goes on in the woods is interesting. And the backwoodsman, even at the present time, when finding himself in need of boiling water and lacking a metal bucket, not infrequently constructs a birch-bark bucket. In doing so, generally speaking, he proceeds as follows:

He finds a good-sized birch tree and strips off a piece of bark about twenty inches wide, making sure that this is fairly free from abrasions and has not clinging to it many of the papery, fluffy curls that are characteristic of the white birch; for these curls are very inflammable. He then folds the strip of bark into the form of an ordinary square package, its top being left open. A splinter is inserted at either end of the box to hold it tight. This is the completed bark bucket.

The woodsman then builds a small stone fireplace topped by two flat rocks, these about two or three inches apart. He starts a fire beneath these and allows it to burn down to hot coals. This stage being reached, he fills his square bark bucket with water, lays this over the opening, straddling the two flat rocks and chinks in on either side of the opening with wet moss or mud so that any flames which spurt up from below will not touch the sides of the bucket. In a surprisingly short time the water comes to a bubbling boil. The bucket will not catch fire so long as water remains in it and the flames do not touch its sides.

Baking potatoes, corn, or eggs in ashes, baking bread either on a hot stone or a stick—these and similar primitive cooking methods prove uncommonly useful at times to the modern camper. The same is true to some extent as regards various utensils connected with the campfire, which we ordinarily do not take along. A certain amount of resourcefulness combined with the forest's bounty fills the need.

For example, suppose that we lack fire-tongs, a broom and a shovel. When the gipsy needs fire-tongs, he finds these in the first pliable green stick that meets his roving eye. After bending the stick in the middle so that the two ends touch, he loops a root or cord around the two legs, half way up and has a serviceable pair of tongs.

The primitive camp broom is the kind that witches in children's story books ride upon— merely a bundle of flexible twigs tied securely to a stick. A fire shovel is made by splitting slightly one end of a stout stick and securing in this clef a sheet of green bark, or, better still, a sheet of tin in case the latter is available.

This simple split-stick principle is one that should be remembered, for it is applicable to numerous camp conveniences. For example, the handle of the camp frying pan (in case this is of city kitchen construction) may be inserted in such a cleft, securely bound, thus making the pan's

Cooking with Nature's Tools 149

handle four or five feet long and enabling the cook to fry his fish without he himself being scorched in the process.

Fire hooks with which to lift hot kettles are essential to most camps. Countless generations ago, some unknown genius of a primitive people discovered that in severing the branch of a tree just below a crotch and then in turn cutting the fork so that one arm was about three of four inches long and the other about twenty inches long, he had an excellent fire hook. And it is just as serviceable a hook to-day as it was then.

A further usefulness of such a hook is that of holding kettles suspended from an overhead crane. In this case, the hook is inverted and the handle of the kettle grips one of a row of notches cut in the handle of the hook.

Sometimes we lose a spoon or two when there is no store at hand from which to replenish the camp supply. There is, however, always a small split stick the length of a spoon handle and by no means infrequently there are shell-fish on the beach. The combination of the stick and a clam shell becomes an excellent spoon. Simply split the stick for about a third of its length, insert one end of the shell in its cleft, and then bind the handle tightly in order to keep the spoon secure.

We live in the twentieth century, of course, and wiesly enough place upon modern cooking utensils our main reliance. Yet we would miss a good bit of the fun of camping were we wholly to disregard the ways of the gipsy and the redskin. If we did, corn roasts, clam-bakes, and "bacon bats" would become a thing of the past. And what a pity that would be.

CHAPTER XI

THE CAMPER'S DISH LIST

COOKING and dining dishes that you take on a camping trip should be simple, useable, adaptable, and durable. This rule is applicable to almost any kind of camping although, of course, there are some types of camping which demand fewer and more compact utensils than do others. One must always be guided in one's selection of dishes by such elements as, the nature and duration of the trip, the number of people who go, the manner in which they go and the sort of cooking fire that is to be used.

For example, any dishes that are breakable are ordinarily wholly out of place, for the dishes of camp life are usually subject to a considerable amount of banging. Yet, this rule is not without its exceptions: either when living in a permanent camp or camping with a motor car, a few glass jars performing service as food containers may prove very convenient.

Another example is the use of enamel-ware cooking dishes. This particular type of ware, while being wholly suitable in the form of camp dining dishes, is not especially well adapted to the purpose of cooking over an open fire. Yet in case one makes use of a camp stove, it may in many instances prove quite suitable.

The best example of how circumstances may alter cases is the matter of compactness. You will find slight resemblance between the cooking kit of the hiker who carries all his belongings on his back, that of the camping motorist whose load is carried for him, and that of the permanent camper who has no load to bother with at all. As Donald Hough aptly remarks in *Outing*:

> If you go light and the fire has no ornaments draped around it and the food is a little different from that to which you have been accustomed, and if the Big Pail is used for beans and rice and carrying water and cooking fish and heating dishwater and boiling soiled shirts . . . then it's a different thing.

In the average home kitchen cupboard there are some cooking and dining dishes which are adapted to average camp life and others which are not. Yet, as regards almost any type of camping, the home kitchen cupboard when peeled down to a happy combination of simplicity and variety may serve as an excellent working model for the selection of one's camp utensils. A survey of its content gives you a very fair idea of what you do need and do not need. Substitutions and eliminations may be made according to the nature of the camping and the number of people that go.

Consider first, the circumstances of average permanent camping. Periodic packing and unpacking of one's belongings are in this case eliminated. You settle in one place, stay there, and wish all the simple conveniences possible; actual living conditions of the home may be largely duplicated. Even so, you have no room for utensils which are not being brought into more or less constant use.

There are a surprisingly large number of cooking and dining dishes that are useable not only at home but also in camp. With a certain amount of substitution and elimination for the sake of simplicity and durability, the utensils of the average permanent camp may be a fairly close duplication of those of the home. In many instances the necessary dishes may be transplanted bodily from home kitchen to camp kitchen. Enamel ware dining dishes serve as a pleasing and unbreakable substitute for fragile china. Life becomes further simplified when the table-cloth is oilcloth.

The average number of people occupying a permanent camp is four. Let us consider such a camping trip, say of one month's duration, presuppose that compactness in packing is no special object and that the cooking will be done with a camp stove having an oven. The following is a list of utensils which will be in more or less constant use in a four-person permanent camp:

KITCHEN UTENSILS

2 Sauce pans (2 quarts each)
2 Cooking kettles (about 5 quart and 10 quart)
2 Steel frying pans
1 Wire broiler (one that won't warp)
1 Double boiler (2 or 3 quart)
1 Coffee pot (2 quart)
3 Baking pans
1 Bean pot
2 Small tin pails
1 Large water pail
1 Colander
1 Measuring cup
1 Tea and coffee strainer
1 Large strainer
1 Skimmer
1 Tea pot or tea ball
1 Flour sifter
1 Rolling pin
1 Bread kneading board
1 Mixing pan
1 Pancake turner
1 Meat fork (large)
2 Cooking spoons (long handled)
1 Carving knife
1 Bread knife
3 Small sharp knives
1 Can opener
1 Corkscrew
1 Whetstone

The Camper's Dish List

1 Egg beater
1 Soup ladle
2 Milk pans
1 Milk can
1 Dipper
5 Pan and kettle covers
3 Pie plates
1 Tray
1 Dish pan
1 Wash basin
1 Meat safe (fly-proof cover)
Soap (2 kinds)
Matches (in bottles or tins)
Dish towels
Dish cloths (wire and cloth)
Cheese cloth (many uses)
Food containers (jars and pry-up cans)
Lid lifter
Wire
Pair of pliers
Oil can
Lantern
Axe
Hatchet
Rope and twine
Shovel

DINING UTENSILS

3 Pitchers (1 large, 2 small)
6 Plates (fairly deep)
6 Cups
5 Saucers
5 Bowls
6 Knives

6 Forks
5 Teaspoons
5 Dessert spoons
3 Tablespoons
3 Serving dishes
Pepper and salt shakers
Paper napkins
Oilcloth cover

In case an open fire and over-head cranes are to be used in place of a camp stove, it may be found advisable to make a few minor changes in the foregoing kitchen-utensil list. Under such circumstances, the side handle of a sauce pan proves something of a bother; over-head bail handles are more convenient. Kettles may be substituted for sauce pans. An ordinary coffee pot may acquire such a handle through the simple process of looping a piece of wire above the cover from handle to spout. Wire is always a convenient adjunct in camping.

The use of a Dutch oven fairly well eliminates the need for baking pans. The same is true as regards the average reflector oven. The milk can and pans may, of course, be eleminated in case you are confined to the use of either canned or powdered milk.

Either strong aluminum ware or unseamed block tin is perhaps a more generally serviceable material for camp cooking vessels than is enamel ware. A block tin utensil is one having a foundation of iron or steel and for this reason a kettle of this sort is much more dependable than is one of ordinary tin. Remember, however, that one must not soak and stew fruits in a tin utensil of any kind. Remember also, that ordinarily a steel frying pan is preferable to one of aluminum.

The foregoing tabulation of kitchen and dining utensils, taken as a whole, represents an allowance that is comfortably liberal for four people and a trifle scant for six. A certain amount of leeway of this sort is usually desirable in permanent camping. Perhaps a couple of friends may drop in for dinner or to spend a week-end. There are enough dishes to go around.

Yet when you begin to count piece by piece the individual utensils in this list you arrive in due time at an appallingly large total. In spite of the fact that these numerous utensils are for the most part confined to ordinary daily needs, there are without doubt altogether too many as regards the comfort both of those who go camping only for a few days and those who have only a limited amount of carrying space.

It becomes necessary in such cases to simplify the list. One manner of accomplishing this consists in making a single utensil serve several purposes. A certain amount of ingenuity goes a long way toward compiling a set of utensils which is at once comparatively few in number and thorough in offering variety in cooking methods.

Thus, the ordinary double boiler may be eliminated. Unfortunately, oatmeal always burns over the campfire unless it is cooked in a double boiler. So, we must devise a double boiler of sorts. Two kettles, one a trifle smaller than the other may in addition to various other uses become a fairly satisfactory double boiler. It is not essential that the rim of the smaller fit snuggly that of the larger. It is, however, advisable to place small stones in the bottom of the larger for the other to rest upon, for otherwise it will bob riotously about.

A few further examples as indicative of the numerous ways in which the utensil list may be cut down when there is need for this are: a bottle becomes an excellent rolling pin, a strip of canvas tacked on a box is a good enough substitute for a bread-kneading board, a dish pan may also be a mixing pan, a can of beans may be readily opened by making two cuts at right angles in its top and bending back the points, pie plates may become serving dishes, pitchers may be eliminated, and other dining utensils kept down to strict needs.

There is another method of simplifying the dish list which is somewhat comparable to eating your cake and having it too; in other words, you can carry with you a fairly large number of dishes,

The Camper's Dish List

these so compactly arranged that they are no special bother. Even in this case, however, one not infrequently finds it an advantage to make a single utensil serve several purposes.

Any "here to-day and away to-morrow" type of camping such as motoring, hiking, or canoeing demands varying degrees of compactness. Packing, unpacking and the carrying of utensils in these instances play an important part in the camper's life. These must be reduced to the most simple terms compatible with comfort or else they may become a constant source of irritation.

Compactness implies utensils which when being transported take up only a fraction as much room as they do when spread out in actual use. This is accomplished through means either of folding or nesting; sometimes both. Packing problems become very much simplified when a dozen utensils of varying sizes from large to small nest one within the other so that you have only one package to carry instead of twelve.

In case ordinary kitchen utensils are chosen, these should be selected with view to their nesting ability in packing arrangements. Such a proceeding not infrequently assumes the aspect of working out a jig-saw puzzle for the reason that not all pieces of ordinary kitchen ware are favored with especially effective nesting or folding capacities. The rim of a certain pot or pan may be bordered by protruding arms, lips, or ears that sturdily object to the nesting of a utensil which is just a trifle smaller.

Through due process of elimination and substitution, it is possible to collect a fairly complete set of ordinary utensils that nest with a reasonable degree of compactness. This usually necessitates a diligent search through sundry kitchen-ware counters, for the possibilities of the home kitchen are as a rule altogether too limited in this respect. Throughout this selection, most utensils having side handles may wisely be eliminated, for side handles are invariably a nuisance in packing arrangements.

The frying-pan handle, for example, may be eliminated and thereby cease to be a source of packing irritation if you buy a pan which is provided either with a detachable or folding handle; in the latter case, when the pan is not in use, the handle is folded back so that it fits flat and is entirely out of the way.

Likewise, the difficulty of packing readily the ordinary wide-based and narrow-top coffee pot is overcome in case you choose the camping type of coffee pot which is built more along the lines of a pail, has a side handle which folds back, and thus nests conveniently within another utensil. A set of cups having the lower ends of their handles detached may be nested within the coffee

The Camper's Dish List 161

pot. Almost any small pail, as a matter of fact, performs able service as a coffee pot.

Various more or less complete nesting-dish outfits that are sold by camping outfitters save one the bother of collecting one's own. There are respective two-person, four-person, and six-person ready prepared kits of this sort. Through courtesy of Abercrombie and Fitch Company an accompanying drawing is given showing the content of

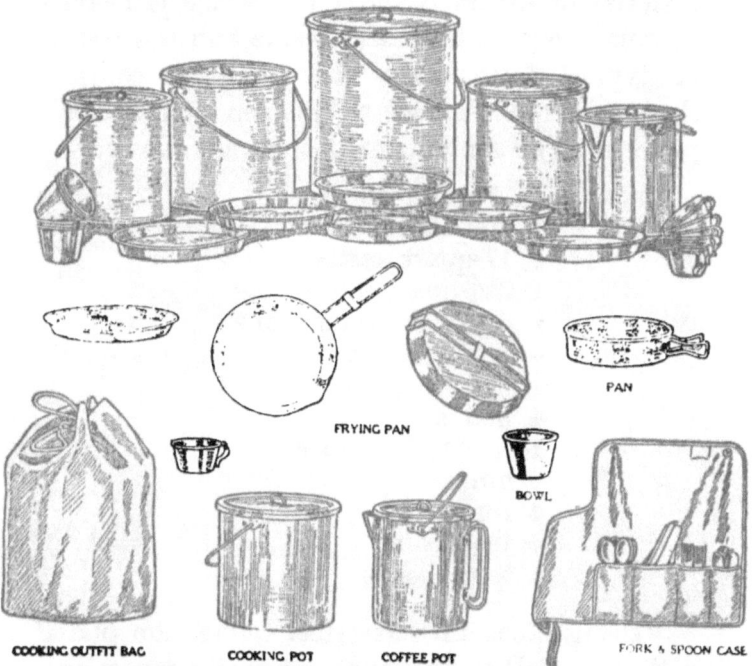

AN EXAMPLE OF A TYPICAL NESTING DISH OUTFIT. ALL THESE UTENSILS, WHEN PACKED, ARE A SINGLE PACKAGE.

a typical set of this sort. I am indebted to this concern for a number of drawings in this book showing equipment.

The various dishes, pots, and pans comprising such a kit nest in such a compact manner that the complete outfit when being transported is only a trifle larger than the size of the largest kettle. Some of these kits are made of aluminum ware and thus are especially light in weight while the material of others is block tin, which is heavier in weight but quite as serviceable and less costly. A typical four-person aluminum set contains thirty-five utensils and weighs ten and one-half pounds. The contents of this are as follows:

- 1 7-quart kettle
- 1 9-quart kettle
- 1 11-quart kettle
- 1 2¼-quart coffee pot
- 2 8½-inch frying pans
- 4 1-pint bowls
- 4 ¾ pint cups
- 4 plates
- 1 salt and pepper
- 4 knives
- 4 forks
- 4 teaspoons
- 4 tablespoons

Various block tin sets (steel foundation plated with tin) follow the same general proportions. Either an aluminum or block tin kit of this order is well adapted to motoring, canoeing, and similar forms of camping which provide some means of transportation. Some campers find it an advantage to substitute enamel-ware plates and cups for aluminum and tin. These and various other substitutions may be made without seriously disrupting the nesting capacities of a given set. Without doubt, enamel-ware cups and a steel frying pan are both preferable to aluminum.

Any camper who has the facilities for carrying one of these sets will probably not be inconvenienced through the addition of several utensils which these sets lack. The kitchen utensil list given for permanent camping will serve as a guide in this respect. Selections may be made according to needs and carrying capacities. Campers who keep more or less on the go do not wish to have too many articles constantly to pack and unpack or these may prove more of an encumbrance than help. Cooking and dining utensils do not gradually vanish as does food. You always have them with you.

The camping hiker is the extreme example of making one utensil serve several purposes and at the same time carrying a cooking kit which is the last word in compactness. Every ounce of strictly unnecessary weight becomes to him just so much unnecessary burden. It would be folly for him to carry more weight or bulk than is essential to his well-being. Yet if he broils with sticks and bakes with his frying pan, he may enjoy with a very limited supply of utensils, a fairly well-rounded program of cooking variety.

Various types of light-weight cooking outfits designed especially for hiking serve very well in this respect. The average weight of a one-man kit of this order is barely two pounds and some of these are sufficiently compact to fit into a coat pocket. My personal liking, however, is for an Army frying pan and two small nesting buckets. Food is carried in the smaller bucket. The following list is suggestive of the utensil needs of two camping hikers:

>   3 Nesting buckets
>   2 Army frying pans
>   2 Knives
>   2 Forks
>   2 Small spoons
>   2 Cups
>   Cheese cloth
>   Small length of wire
>   Dish towel
>   Matches
>   Soap

In brief explanation of the foregoing; one bucket should always be enamel ware or some material other than tin in order that fruit may be soaked and stewed in it. The lids of the frying

The Camper's Dish List 165

pans serve as plates. An old tin can which you sometimes have the good fortune to find, after being burned out and scoured, may become an additional utensil through the acquirement of a wire handle.

The vacuum bottle is a piece of dining equipment demanding some manner of attention in the present chapter. This effective means of keeping food hot for a number of hours after it has left the fire is more closely associated with motoring than any other type of camping. As a rule, when touring, one does not care to unpack camping equipment and build a fire for the noon meal. A more convenient arrangement is that of putting up a lunch at breakfast time. Yet when noon comes, one is usually very grateful for the presence of hot coffee or even hot food in the lunch.

Vacuum bottles are of two general types. One of these is the pint or quart affair having a narrow mouth; the use of this is confined to a liquid such as coffee or tea. Of various bottles of this particular type I recommend especially a certain variety of bottle which is unbreakable. This is built entirely of steel, with the result that if you drop it from car to pavement it continues to remain in good working order.

The second general type of vacuum bottle takes up a greater amount of space and weighs more than does the first, but its sphere of usefulness is more extensive in that it has a capacity of a gallon or more and has a three- or four-inch-wide mouth which permits the entrance of food. This large vacuum bottle, shaped something after the order of a jug, is really a food jar, although it may be used for keeping hot either solid food or liquids.

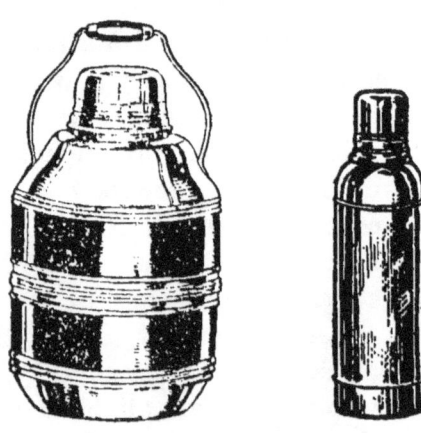

A VACUUM FOOD JAR AND VACUUM BOTTLE.

Any vacuum bottle, of course, has the accommodating habit of turning about face and keeping its contents cold instead of hot when cold food is what you wish. Hence, the usefulness of a vacuum food jar as an ice-box of sorts. After being chilled, it will keep in good condition for many hours, say, a pint bottle of cream and a pound of butter. But in such a case, remember to wrap and pack the bottle of cream so that no glass will be broken. Various other methods of keeping food fresh are described in Chapter **XVII.**

CHAPTER XII

CAMP CRANES AND FIRES

THE camp kettle that turns a fire-smothering hand-spring into the embers is one of the familiar dark little tragedies of cooking over an open fire. A slight amount of ingenuity in the form of erecting some sort of substantial camp crane will, however, obviate such a tragedy. The absence of a camp stove providing a solid base is taken for granted. The use of a stove may largely obviate the need for a crane.

A crane is either a single stick or an arrangement of several sticks suspended above the fire in such a position that the kettle may dangle from its support and simmer safely and cheerfully in the rising heat.

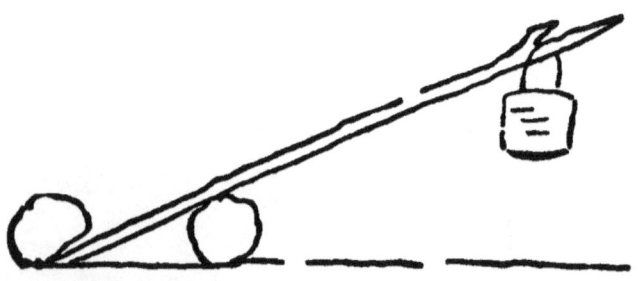

A SINGLE-STICK CRANE. IT CAN BE RAISED OR LOWERED BY MOVING THE FORWARD ROCK.

Camp Cranes and Fires 169

The most serviceable type of single-stick crane is, as a rule, one which can be readily lowered or raised during the process of cooking so that the kettle dangling from its end receives the exact degree of heat which it requires. The following may be taken as general instructions for the building of such a crane:

Trim a green stick to a length of about six feet and shove this into the ground at an angle of about forty-five degrees to the ground surface in such a position that the upper end of this slanting stick is above the fire.

Place either a hefty rock or a good-sized log under the stick about a foot or two toward the fire from the buried end; this will prevent the crane from bending too low or falling down when a heavy kettle is hung upon its fire end. Place another rock or log on the ground above the buried end of the crane as a safeguard against its pulling out from the earth socket.

Cut a notch or drive a couple of nails in the upper side of the crane at a point directly above the fire. Either arrangement will hold the handle of the kettle in place and prevent it from slipping off. Notches for additional kettles can be cut in case the stick is sufficiently stout to hold these. And then, your simple single-stick crane is complete.

The fire in its early stages is likely to be high

and flaring, a condition which makes it advisable to allow the kettle to swing rather high. But as the flames begin to simmer down, you can lower the kettle accordingly. This is accomplished by the simple process of moving forward the rock

USING A CROTCHED STICK FOR SINGLE-CRANE SUPPORT.

or log located under the slanting crane. On the other hand, by moving the rock or log backward, away from the fire, you raise the crane; and up with it goes the kettle.

A number of variations of this single-stick crane principle are possible. For example, a crotched stick is sometimes substituted for the supporting rock or log. Again, the crane instead of being planted in the ground may be in a horizontal position, wholly off from the ground.

This arrangement consists of the crane and two crotched sticks, the latter being driven into the ground several inches apart. The crotch farthest from the fire is inverted and the far end of the crane is hooked under this. The other crotch points upward in its normal way and thus, at this point, holds up the crane. The fire is beyond, under the end of the crane, as in the case of the previously described device. A large rock, of course, may give the same support as does the crotch nearest the fire. There are no fixed rules as regards construction. One must be guided largely by natural conditions.

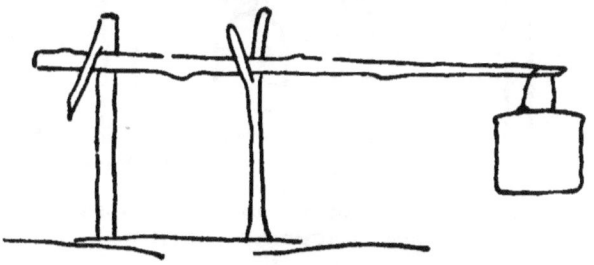

SOMETIMES A SINGLE CRANE OF THIS TYPE IS CONVENIENT.

For example, when building a fire against a vertical rock or bank, you can sometimes shove one end of a stick into a crevice directly above the fire. And you have a perfectly workable crane. Or, in case such an opening is lacking, perhaps the crane will remain solidly in place by the addition of a heavy rock upon its end.

None of the foregoing types of cranes is especially well adapted to the work of holding several kettles at the same time. The most generally useful arrangement of this sort is a horizontal crane supported by two crotched sticks, but in this instance with the fire between the sticks instead of being off at one side after the manner just mentioned.

THE MOST GENERALLY USEFUL CRANE ARRANGEMENT FOR HOLDING A NUMBER OF KETTLES.

When woodsmen build a crane of this type, they select crotched sticks which are about four feet long and two inches in diameter. Each of these is driven vertically into the ground at either end of the fire so that they are three or four feet apart. Frequently, an open fire-place either of rocks or logs or a combination of both, is built as well. The horizontal crane is laid upon the supporting crotches so that it is directly over the fire and about three feet above it. The kettles are permitted to dangle from this crane crosspiece.

To hang the handles of the kettles directly upon

the crane itself is not very satisfactory. Successful cooking operations demand some arrangement whereby the kettles may dangle at varying heights; they should be allowed to follow up and down the flickering fortunes of the fire. Furthermore, it would be extremely troublesome to be forced to lift up one end of the crane every time you wished either to put on or take off a kettle.

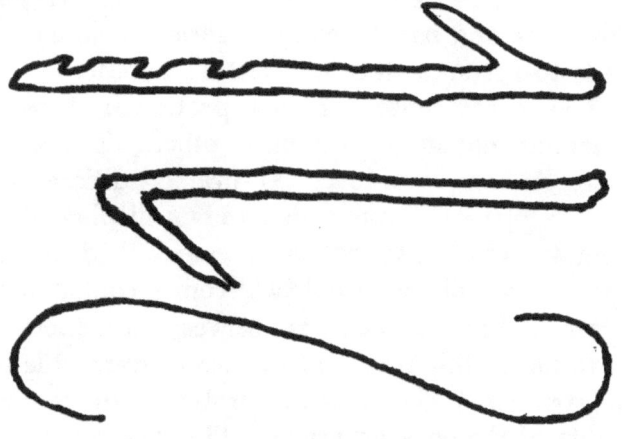

CONVENIENT TYPES OF POT-HOOKS, CROTCHED STICKS AND WIRE.

A pot-hook, having the shape of an elongated letter S, proves of great value in this connection; the bottom of the S grasps the kettle handle while the top circles the crane. A collection of hooks of this sort of varying lengths is advisable. You can make them by clipping off several pieces of strong wire and bending these into the right shapes.

A small wire chain having a catch attached at either end serves the same purpose and in some respects is even more convenient than the pothooks in that the chain may be readily lengthened or shortened. Far back in the woods the most usual sort of pot-hook used is the type mentioned in Chapter X; an inverted wood crotch gripping the crane and having either a series of notches or nails to accommodate the kettle's handle.

The construction of this particular type of crane, in common with most others, is open to more or less variation. Natural conditions in a certain place sometimes demands a display of ingenuity which may not be so essential in another spot. The following extract from a contributor's letter to *Field and Stream* serves as an excellent example of this fact. The letter concerns the use of straight sticks, without crotches for the uprights of the cooking crane. The writer says:

I was camping with a guide in a pine country where crotches are hard to find, the pine trees, large and small, growing straight to the sky. But this didn't bother him at all.

The first night out and every night thereafter he felled a small pine about two inches at the base and cut three sticks from it. Two of them were about three and one-half feet, the third, four or

Camp Cranes and Fires 175

five feet. The two he sharpened and drove into the ground, one at either side of where the cook fire was to be and three or four feet apart.

He then flattened both ends of the other, deftly

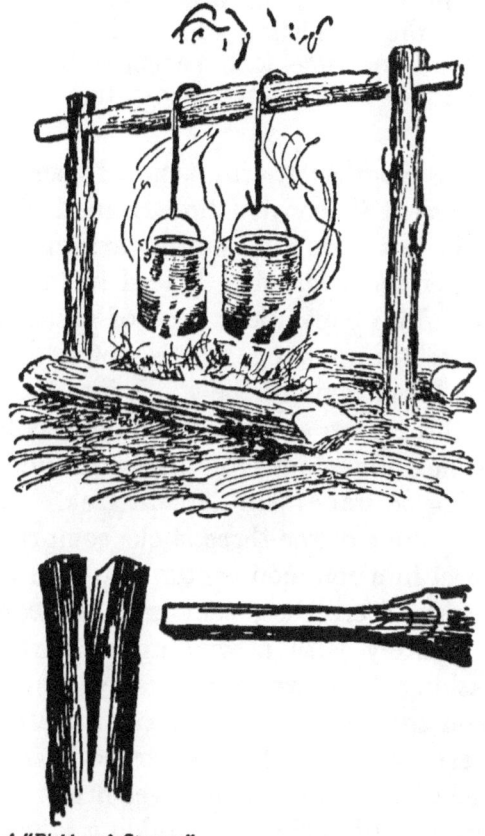

Courtesy of "Field and Stream."

THE "SPLIT-STICK" CRANE, VALUABLE WHEN CROTCHED STICKS ARE UNAVAILABLE.

split the tops of the uprights and inserted the flattened ends. The crane was built easily, quickly, and securely.

There are times and places where the crotched stick crane would be the best, but for most fires I consider the split stick superior. Most important, there is no time lost searching for crotches, and no danger of breaking them when driving the sticks.

There is another useful type of camp crane, quite different in construction from those so far described, this being a simple arrangement of three sticks above the fire, braced in the form of a tripod. This convenient type of crane literally becomes self-supporting. It is not necessary to drive the lower ends of the sticks into the ground and for this reason a crane of this particular type has distinct advantages on rocky ground where the driving of stakes is a difficult task.

The top ends of the three sticks comprising this crane meet in a common center. In case the ends are devoid of crotches, they may be bound together securely with a winding of wire. This wire lashing becomes unnecessary, however, if when you cut the sticks you leave a crotch at the end of each. Then, when the crane is assembled, the three crotches lock themselves firmly together.

Campers ordinarily in building this tripod crane cut the three legs so that these are all of the same length. The result may be a workable and sturdy device in case only a limited amount of cooking space is required. With this arrangement, however, there is hardly room for more than one kettle to dangle over the fire.

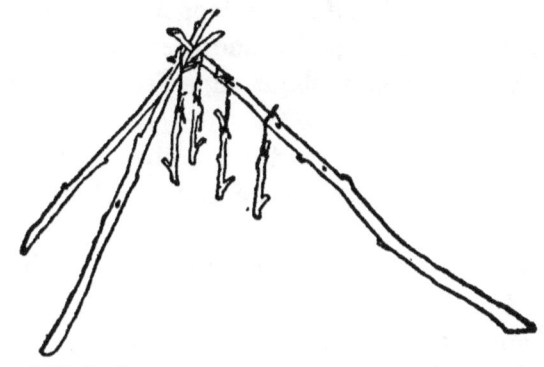

Courtesy of "Outing."

AN EFFECTIVE TRIPOD CRANE.

I learned from Frederic Baxter some years ago the useful trick of having one of the legs of the tripod longer than the other two. If you cut two of the sticks of equal length and the remaining stick three or four feet longer than these, you will then have in the completed crane sufficient room for hanging a number of kettles from it at the same time. For, in this case, the center of the fire is not directly under the meeting point of the sticks; it is a trifle to one side, under the upper third of the longest leg of the tripod.

A row of chains, pot-hooks, or inverted crotches with kettles attached may be hung along the length of this slanting leg. Nails can be driven or notches cut in the upper side of the leg to accommodate pot-hooks. Even strong pieces of cord attached to the hooks and tied over the leg may be used. Satisfactory lengths for the respective legs of this tripod crane are: six feet for the two short legs and about nine feet for the long leg.

In building any sort of crane, green wood, when available, should be used. Dry wood is likely to catch fire.

The camp crane belongs essentially to the open fire. Its usefulness vanishes when you make use of a stove and the fire becomes imprisoned by a top lid, for then you set the kettles on the lid. But so long as the top remains open, the crane in one form or another may prove a valuable adjunct to camp cooking.

In the chapter which follows, for example, there are described various types of camp fireplaces. In several instances, a camp crane may to advantage be used in conjunction with these.

But we're putting the cart before the horse. What of the fire? Its magic fragrance and curling smoke are not always earned with ease. Some people do not have very good luck in building and starting a campfire. There's a good bit in method. Ordinarily, one cannot carelessly dump an armful of sticks on the ground, touch a match to it, and expect the pile to burn. Even though a tiny blaze does start, it may presently be smothered to death. One must use method.

There are various ways of building a fire, but in each case the same fundamental principles of getting action hold true. One of these is: the natural movement of a flame is upward. Hence, the desirability of lighting the wood close to the ground. When the wind is blowing, however, the natural movement of a flame is both upward and forward. So, in this case the fire should be lighted near the ground on the windward side of the pile.

Concurrently with the upward movement, a young flame demands plenty of air circulation. Unless air circulates freely along the bottom of the pile and all through it upward, the flame will presently die. Therefore, the undesirability of piling on very much wood until the flame has taken a firm hold, for this action blocks the free passage of air and smothers the flame. Similarly, heavier wood above the kindling should be so arranged that it will not crash down and put out the ambitious fire.

A third fundamental principle of fire building is as follows: wet wood will not burn. Wet wood, to be sure, becomes dry in a remarkably short time after coming into contact with a reasonable amount of heat. But it is quite essential that you have dry wood with which to start the fire. The wet wood when added dries automatically.

The gathering of dry kindling during rainy weather is sometimes a problem, although diligent search for pieces that have remained dry in spite of the rain invariably brings results. For example, the under side of a leaning dead tree and the core of an old stump may each present dry offerings. And when your precious find is gathered: keep it dry. In case rain is coming down, hold your coat over the young crackling flame until it is well started. After that it will probably be able to take care of itself. During very heavy rain, however, it is advisable to construct a simple lean-to of sticks sheltering the fire.

The most generally satisfactory type of fire for cooking purposes in connection with the use of camp cranes and also with open fireplaces is a small fire built in the form of a cone. The foundation consists of slivers of kindling arranged in cone formation around a wad of paper, shavings, or similar inflammable material. Bordering the slivers in the same fashion with their top ends meeting in a common center is a row of larger sized kindling. As previously indicated, care must be taken not to block the free passage of air. When the fire gets under way, as many more sticks can be leaned against the cone-like structure as the occasion demands.

Camp Cranes and Fires 181

The Indians, when building a fire of this sort, make a practise of having as a foundation several sticks arranged on the ground in the form of the spokes of a wheel. Thus the point of the cone comes directly above the hub. This is an effective measure in case the fire is wholly in the open. Another variation of the cone idea is a pig-pen-like structure of sticks bordered by another row of sticks leaning against this and meeting in a common center, the fire getting its start upon smaller material in the hollow pig-pen square.

First, last, and all time, when a campfire is built, thought should be given to the possibility of its spreading and setting fire to the woods. One cannot be too cautious in this respect. According to U. S. Forest Service estimates, more than one-third of the total number of devastating fires on the National Forests of this country originate from the inexperience or carelessness of campers.

Because of being in unaccustomed surroundings, failure of many campers to realize the ease with which a forest fire may be started and the terrible havoc it leaves, is without doubt the reason for such a condition. A forest floor during a dry spell is like a tinder box. Even the dropping of an unextinguished cigarette has started devastating fires. Curiously enough, it is sometimes a more simple matter to start a forest fire than it is to make a campfire. Doubtless, the difficulty experienced by some campers in getting a campfire under way blinds them to the possibility of its spreading when once started.

Among the basic rules which the Forest Service gives for the prevention of forest fires are the following:

Never build a campfire against a tree or log, in leaf mold or in rotten wood. Build all fires away from overhanging branches and on a dirt or rock foundation. Dig out all rotten wood or leaf mold from the fire pit and scrape away all inflammable material within a radius of from three to five feet. Make sure the fire cannot spread on or under the ground or up the moss or bark of a tree while you are in camp and that it is going to be easy to extinguish when you are ready to leave.

Never leave a campfire, even for a short time, without completely extinguishing every spark with water or fresh dirt free from moss and leaf mold. Do not throw charred cross logs to one side where a smoldering spark might catch. It is well to soak thoroughly all embers and charred pieces of wood and then cover them with dirt. Feel around the outer edge of the fire pit to make sure no fire is smoldering in charred roots or leaf mold. Hundreds of fires escape each year after campers have thought they were extinguished.

In brief, make sure that a fire is cold before you leave it.

CHAPTER XIII

OUT-OF-DOORS FIREPLACES

THE materials that go into the construction of a camp fireplace and its utensil-holding props may be wood, rock, earth, or metal. Sometimes you make use of a combination of two or three of these materials.

There are a good many different ways of building an outdoor fireplace. The exact method which you may find most suitable under certain conditions is dependent largely upon such elements as the natural or mechanical facilities at hand and whether you are in a hurry or have plenty of time. For this reason, there are advantages in being familiar with several methods.

The term "camp fireplace" usually implies a structure of some sort which encloses two or three sides of the fire. Such an arrangement, so far as cooking purposes are concerned, is, as a rule, preferable to having a fire wholly in the open in that the heat is fairly well confined to the business of cooking instead of being distributed broadcast. A given amount of fuel lasts longer in a fireplace than in the open, and furthermore, the use of a confined fire usually lessens distinctly the chances of setting fire to one's surroundings.

Two green logs on the ground parallel to each other with the fire built in between is one type of fireplace. Green sticks or metal rods spanning the breech between the logs may serve as props for pots and pans. A crane, either of the single-stick or horizontal variety, may be used in conjunction with this arrangement in case there is need for it.

Sometimes you will find it advisable to lay your two green logs on the ground in the shape of a V, the respective ends nearly although not quite touching at one end and being about twenty inches apart at the other. In case the upper sides of the logs are first flattened with an axe, these will serve as convenient rests for cooking utensils. Even so, metal rods spanning the opening are more reliable as supports.

The two logs should be laid on the ground so that the wide end of the V faces the wind. This gives the proper draught. It is sometimes worth while to bank earth against the outer sides of the logs both in order to keep them from rolling and to seal up undesirable draughts.

A log fireplace of the general sort just described serves only as temporary expedient. For, as the green wood gradually becomes dried out from the heat, it is likely to catch fire. And then you have no more fireplace. Furthermore, a fireplace of

Out-of-Doors Fireplaces 185

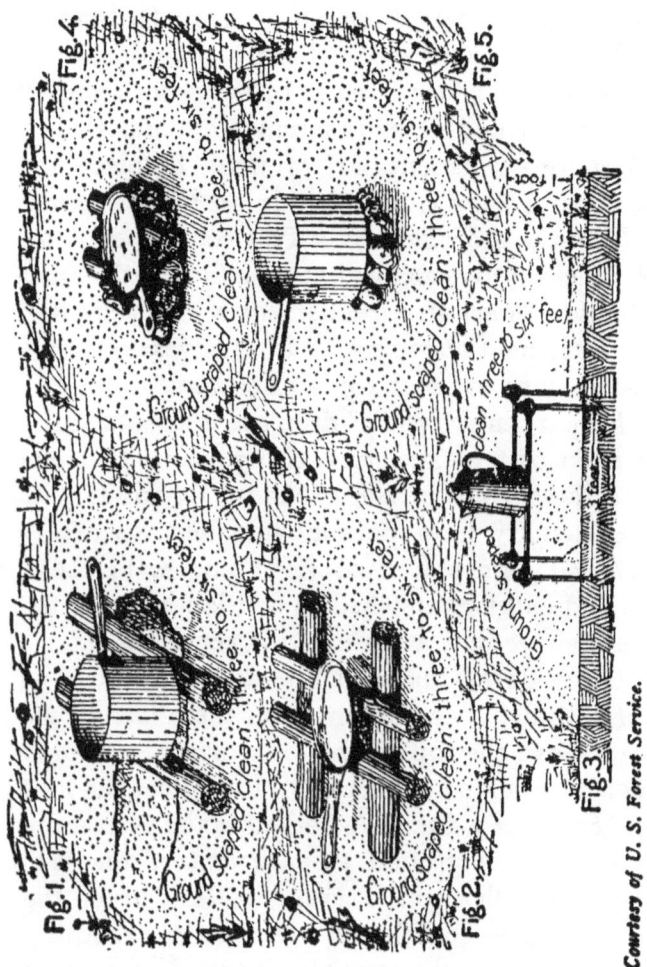

Courtesy of U. S. Forest Service.

A FEW METHODS OF BUILDING A SIMPLE FIREPLACE. THE USE OF FIRE-IRONS IS SHOWN BELOW.

this type is sometimes a good bit of a risk as regards the danger of spreading fire. Ordinarily, the Forest Service would hardly countenance it. Its use should be confined to open spaces removed from timber and other inflammable material.

A more permanent sort of wood fireplace and also a safer type is one that is used quite extensively in the Adirondacks. This consists of a low crib of green logs chinked and padded with stones and mud. Such an arrangement serves very well for permanent camping, but involves rather a large amount of labor for a brief stay.

This particular type of fireplace is a rectangular log-cabin sort of structure rising about two feet above the surface of the ground. In addition to the customary long parallel side logs, there are short end logs placed at right angles to these. Side and end logs notched to overlap in much the same manner that a log cabin is constructed.

The inside of this crib all the way around is lined with flat rocks set on edge; these loom some inches above the top of the crib. Layers of mud or earth are added, which serve to protect the logs from catching a-fire. A forked stake is usually driven into the ground at each end of the fireplace and a horizontal crane is laid upon the crotches. Green sticks or metal rods straddling the sides of the crib may also be used as sources of utensil support.

Out-of-Doors Fireplaces 187

Every outdoors person has cause sooner or later to build a stone fireplace. There are numerous variations of this type of structure. Two flat

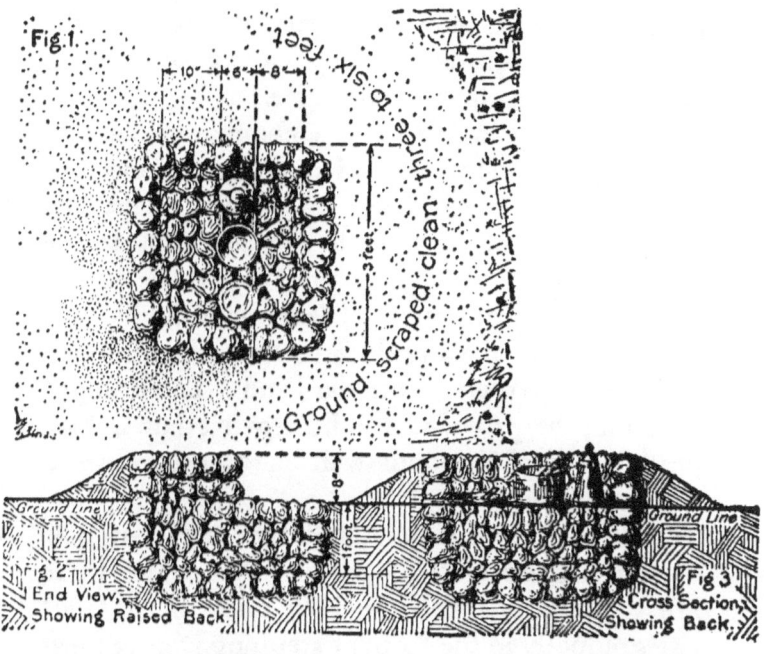

Courtesy of U. S. Forest Service.

TOP, END AND FRONT VIEW OF A TYPE OF STONE FIREPLACE USED BY THE FOREST SERVICE.

rocks on the ground a few inches apart with a pan or pot perched a-top these and a fire underneath is a fireplace of sorts. This simple arrangement becomes more heat conserving, however, if you block one of its open ends with a third rock; a serviceable enough device for the hiker who carries only one or two cooking utensils and wishes a hurried lunch. In case flat rocks are scarce and cobble-stones are abundant, you can arrange the latter in the form of a circle, leaving an opening at one point in its circumference.

With plenty of flat rocks about, one usually likes to go to the trouble of building a stone fireplace that will house fairly good-sized sticks. In doing so, it is worth while to pay attention to the direction of the prevailing wind and then, during the course of construction, leave a draught vent at the back of the fireplace in line with its open end. The open end faces the wind. The draught vent may be provided for by leaving out a rock near the top of the stone-wall-like structure which is your finished fireplace.

Such a structure may be either a rectangular or semicircular wall of rocks. Sometimes there are advantages in having both sides of its front rise gradually in the form of stepping stones; these steps become convenient props for utensils. At other times, there is no need for these. In case you can lay hands upon an old piece of sheet iron you have in this an excellent lid which serves both as a utensil prop and a means for keeping the heat of the fire properly confined. A flat rock may perform like service passably well. If the top is left open, a crane in conjunction with the fireplace is likely to prove of value.

Gipsies, during their many centuries of outdoor living, have learned many things that are likely to be helpful to the modern camper. One of these is the heat-holding property of rock. When the gipsy is about to build a cooking fire, he usually digs a slight depression in the ground, studs this with a layer of stones, and builds the fire on top of the stones, knowing that the presence of this foundation means a hotter fire than does an earth bottom.

Although the gipsy seldom makes use of a stone fireplace, his rock foundation idea can to advantage be used in connection with such a structure. Oftentimes you will find it convenient to arrange your fireplace either upon or around a rock slab.

There is another form of stone foundation, however, offering added usefulness which seems not to have occured to the gipsy. This consists of having the stones perform service as an incinerator for garbage, later thrown into the fire. You first dig a pit about twenty inches deep, two or three feet wide, and about three or four feet long, and fill this to the surface of the ground with loose stones. The fireplace is built upon this foundation. When garbage is emptied upon the fire, the liquid part trickles through the rocks and evaporates.

The average stone fireplace is constructed upon a level with the ground. This location necessitates a considerable amount of crouching and bending-over on the part of the cook tending the fire. The elimination of this more or less constant action

A FIREPLACE OF THIS TYPE IS SOMETIMES WORTH WHILE FOR A PERMANENT CAMPER. IT SAVES BENDING OVER.

may prove a comfort although, of course, the presence of a fireplace several feet above the ground surface likewise eliminates the possibility of the incinerator just described.

Perhaps the lay of the land will permit you to build your fireplace above the ground. There may be close by a large flat-topped boulder about waist high upon which the fireplace can be constructed conveniently. Or lacking this, possibly there is a steep embankment either having a natural shelf or in which a shelf may be readily dug. Lacking all such possibilities, you can build a rectangular rock pier about three feet high and have the fireplace a-top this.

Let us now go to the opposite extreme and examine the possibilities of an earth fireplace. This type of fireplace in its most simple form is merely a round hole in the ground about one foot deep and three feet in diameter. That part of the circle facing the wind is shoveled away in order to provide a draught. Green sticks placed across the hole may serve as supports for pots and pans.

A TRENCH FIREPLACE HAVING A SHEET-METAL LID AND CLAY CHIMNEY.

A more efficient underground fireplace, as a rule, is one having the form of a long narrow trench. This hole may be about five feet long, two feet wide, and one foot deep. Then, if you can locate an old piece of sheet iron conforming in a general way to the first two of these dimensions, you have in this a fortunate find, for it becomes an excellent top lid. Upon this will sit sundry sizzling cooking utensils while the fire crackles within the trench. The lid is upon a level with the surface of the ground. It may be supported by two or three metal bars straddling the sides of the trench.

One end of the trench is left open and through this you feed in the wood. This open end faces the prevailing wind and hence permits the fanning of the fire and the escape of smoke in the proper direction. The smoke's channel of escape may perferably be an old piece of stove-pipe towering above the far end of the trench. The pipe is held solidly in place by a mound which is a mixture of small rocks and clay or mud. Cavities at this end of the fireplace through which smoke and heat might escape are chinked with this mixture.

As previously indicated, a dirt floor in a fireplace is not so efficient as a stone floor. Either a cobble-stone or flat stone bottom may be readily built in if one thinks it worth the trouble. Stone sides may be added in the same manner. Indeed, in localities where the soil is of loose and sandy texture, stone sides are distinctly advisable, for without these acting as supports the dirt sides of the fireplace may topple in.

In case the sheet iron and the stove-pipe are unavailable, you can perhaps use a flat rock as a lid and build a chimney either of stones or clay. Or again, either an old iron bucket after its bottom has been knocked out or a discarded milk can may become a chimney.

Details aside, you doubtless see the general principles of this simple underground fireplace and why it is capable of giving exceptionally good cooking action. It is in all essentials patterned after an up-and-going kitchen range. The heat is confined almost wholly to the business of cooking.

Furthermore, this underground fire is, as a general rule, safer than the average above-ground campfire with sparks scattering broadcast. This, however, does not alter the fact that we must use wise judgment concerning fire risk when digging a trench which is especially rooty and dry. One of the most insidious types of forest fires is the kind that travels underground for many yards by means of decayed vegetation.

As a general rule, the more successful any type of fireplace is as a cooking instrument, the less successful it is from the standpoint of campfire cheerfulness. Thus, as one extreme, we have the highly efficient trench fireplace, which is to all intents a stove and for this reason not the sort of thing that you sit around and admire, and, as the other extreme, we have the cheerful wide open campfire. Several varieties of fireplaces described in the foregoing may perhaps be classified as compromises between these two.

Because of the cheerfulness of the wide open fire there are some campers who in their cooking operations dispense entirely with a fireplace. Convenient hangers and props for utensils under such circumstances are cranes, fire-irons, and folding grates. Each of these can also be used in conjunction with most fireplaces and one sometimes finds it an advantage in this connection to carry along either a set of fire-irons or a grate.

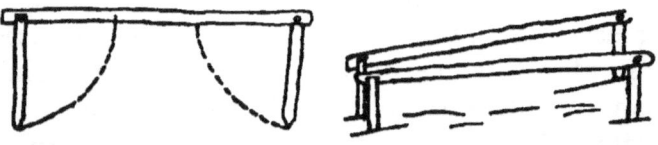

Courtesy of "Outing."

A FIRE-IRON HAVING FOLDING LEGS. DRAWING AT RIGHT SHOWS IRONS PLANTED IN FORM OF A V INSTEAD OF PARALLEL.

Camp fire-irons operate upon the same general principle as do andirons in a home fireplace with the exception that they hold cooking utensils instead of logs. You can make a fire-iron by taking a thin iron rod about four feet long, bending each end at right angles, and then sharpening these with a file so that they may readily enter the ground. These upright ends should each be about six inches long.

Two of these irons are planted in the ground,

side by side over the spot where the fire is to be. Thus, the horizontal bars upon which the utensils rest are four or five inches above the surface of the ground. Both bars must be exactly the same height above the ground or else the utensils will not rest evenly. It is not necessary, however, that the bars be parallel. In fact, it is advisable to have them form something of a V, for in this way the coffee pot and similar narrow based utensils are placed upon the narrow end of the structure while the frying pan and other wide-based pots and pans straddle the wider parts of the chasm.

So far as packing convenience is concerned, there are advantages in carrying fire-irons having legs which either fold or are detachable. For example, Albert Andrews tells of having had a blacksmith make for him a pair of irons from old wagon tires. The legs were separate pieces bolted to the ends so that when not in use they folded in line with the horizontal bar.

A detachable device possible with thin iron rods consists of having separate legs; and the ends both of the legs and horizontal bars bent into the form of rings so that the two may be readily connected. Another possibility is that of carrying two pieces of iron piping having detachable right-angled elbow supports fitting into each open end.

The camp grate in one form or another oftentimes proves an uncommonly convenient adjunct to camp cooking. This popular utensil prop in its most simple form is a rectangular-shaped wire gridiron having a folding leg at each corner. Although primarily designed as a resting place for sizzling pots and pans, it may in addition do service as a broiler. Sometimes it has ready-attached metal sides, but in such instances it becomes a stove. This particular device, together with other types of camp stoves will be described in the following chapter.

The presence in camp both of a grate and a set of fire-irons means a certain amount of duplication. When preparing to cook with either of these, you can oftentimes make use of a crane as well. A high-flaring fire is unsuitable for broiling or frying activities, but may be perfectly so for boiling, in case the kettle is hung from above. Thus, you start the kettle of water on its bubbling way and when in due time the fire has burned down to hot coals, you place the remaining utensils on either the fire-irons or grate, a few inches above the coals.

Remember at all times—in cooking either with a fire-place or a wide open fire—that an extraordinary amount of care should be taken from the standpoint of fire risk, especially so in the case of the latter. During very dry times and when the wind blows hard, an open fire should not be used at all. Remember also the Forest Service rule as regards the construction of fireplaces: scrape the ground clean for a distance of from three to six feet in all directions from the spot where the fireplace is to be built.

CHAPTER XIV

CAMP STOVES

ALMOST any type of out-of-doors fireplace is, to some extent, a stove. Its presence, ordinarily, removes the need for a metal stove. Yet, in case one has ample means of transporting a ready-made camp stove, this is likely to prove uncommonly convenient. Any sort of camping, however, in which such a stove shows indications of becoming a burden, is another matter. In this instance the stove may readily develop into a nuisance.

An average metal camp stove, although neither a thing of beauty nor so cheerful as an open fire, is, none the less, extremely efficient in its all-purposeful object of cooking an out-of-doors meal. This rite is accomplished with a minimum amount of bother to the camper, and when he pulls up stakes to move on to other parts, the stove, as a rule, displays an amiable capacity for folding into a bundle which can be conveniently packed out of people's way in almost any motor car. Camp stoves are especially popular both with migratory motorists and campers who remain for a long time in one site.

Camp Stoves

Metal camp stoves are miniature kitchen ranges. The fuel upon which they feed is in some cases wood, again it is gasoline, while still again it may be either kerosene or alcohol. The wood-burning stove corresponds in a general way to an ordinary coal range, while the gasoline camp stove is somewhat comparable to a city home gas range.

Camp outfitting firms sell many different kinds of wood-burning camp stoves. Most of these fall into one of two classifications. In one case, the fire is only partially enclosed by the stove, while in the other it is wholly enclosed. I will describe first the semi-open type of stove.

If you were to eliminate from an extra large cardboard shoebox its top, bottom, and one end, and then replace the top with a rectangular wire grate you would have a general idea of what a typical stove of this sort looks like. The end and two sides are three plates of sheet metal arranged in the form of a rectangle. The outfit, fundamentally, is merely an ordinary camp grate with a solid metal fence built around it. These plates, as a rule, are detachable.

The size of the stove when set up for cooking is about eleven inches by twenty inches, which offers sufficient room on top of the grate for two or three utensils. Some stoves have an undergrate, as well, upon which the fire is built, while in the case of others, the fire is laid upon the ground. With either arrangement, a small hole poked in the ground under one side or end gives the draught which all stoves require and, in this particular instance, permits a fair amount of regulation of the fire. The stove, when packed for carrying, folds flat to a package of approximately the dimensions just given and only about one inch thick.

The foregoing is a brief summary of perhaps a half dozen makes of this semi-open type of stove. Individual features which some of these may possess are not as a rule of any great importance, so long as the material is sheet steel, as it is in most cases. Sheet iron is likely to warp, and when you try to fold properly a warped folding stove you have on your hands a balky problem.

Most stoves of this type have facilities for baking and roasting. Such an arrangement is a distinct asset. There may be attached to the outer side of one of the side plates a detachable reflector oven which is large enough to accommodate a good-sized roast. The reflector-oven idea is described in detail in the next chapter. With this addition you have in such an outfit every facility for cooking an all-around hearty meal with a stove which is an efficient and practicable compromise between the wide-open campfire and the usual tightly closed box stove.

A stove of this semi-open type is likely to appeal

to campers who may tolerate a high metal fence around their cheerful campfire, but who object to its complete imprisonment. We like to watch the lingering embers slyly wink. Yet if we wish to get along with a lesser amount of fuel and in case we wish to keep our pots and pans free from soot, we can to advantage turn to the type of stove in which the fire is wholly enclosed.

When you use a stove having the fire tightly enclosed in a black little box with a stove-pipe at one end and a door at the other, you can regulate that fire in any manner that suits your fancy— an obvious advantage in cooking. And, of knockdown camp box stoves of this nature there is a small multitude.

As regards my personal choice in the matter, if I wish the convenience of a metal camp stove and planned to camp for quite a long time in one spot, I should be inclined toward a box stove of the general sort just indicated. I should examine a dozen different makes and sizes of these and select the one which seemed capable of duplicating most closely the work of the kitchen range at home.

If I were hiking or canoeing, I should build my own stoves beside trail and stream. If I were camping with a motor car and more or less on the go, I should do the same on occasion, but I should also have with me either a wood-burning stove of the semi-open type or a gasoline stove. Only if I planned to make fairly permanent stops would I be tempted by a box stove. This, however, does not alter the fact that this type of stove is used more or less extensively by motorists who are constantly on the go. Perhaps if I wanted a box stove of sorts for temporary use, I could locate an old tin box, iron bucket, or milk can, and with the application of a little ingenuity have one.

The typical collapsible box stove is fairly small in its dimensions and folds to packing proportions when not in use. In some cases there is an advantage in having a large stove. This is equally obtainable; they are made in all sizes. The box stove usually has a stove-pipe, this as a rule being telescopic so that several two-foot lengths of piping consume a carrying space of but a single length. I recall, however, seeing one stove having a square stove-pipe that folded flat.

The material of which the box stove is made may be variously sheet iron, sheet steel, and cast iron. Sheet iron, as I have previously remarked, is likely to warp with intense heat and therefore give trouble. Cast iron is excellent although heavy. Sheet steel is the most generally suitable material because of its combination of comparative lightness in weight and durability. In case weight were no object, I should be inclined toward cast

Camp Stoves 203

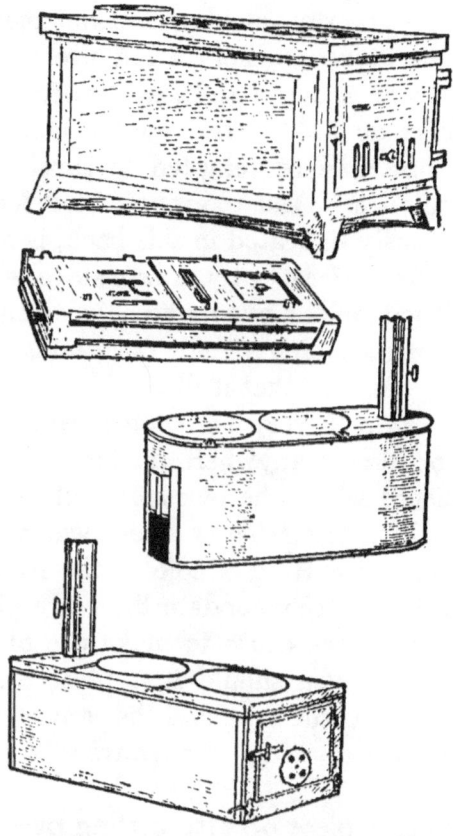

ABOVE: A CAST-IRON BOX STOVE SET UP AND FOLDED.
BELOW: TWO TYPES OF SHEET METAL STOVES.

iron. The weights of various kinds of knock-down stoves range from fifteen to fifty pounds.

When selecting a stove of this sort, one should

examine its capabilities for handling a well-rounded program of cooking and not merely because of its ability to hold a hot fire. Some of these stoves have ovens and facilities for broiling, while others do not. Through the lack of such facilities, one may be tempted to subsist largely upon fried food. And too much fried food, as I have previously indicated in this book, is not good for one. Not infrequently, a box stove which has been built without an oven may acquire one in the form of a detachable reflector oven hung upon its side. Only, be sure that it fits.

If you camp in very high altitudes during the summer or almost anywhere during the late fall, a convenience which the box stove offers in addition to cooking is service as a tent warmer. This necessitates the cutting a hole in the roof of the tent in order to accommodate the stove-pipe. In case you ever have cause to make use of a stove in this respect, you should first place a sheet of asbestos between the pipe and the canvas, for with this safeguard lacking, the canvas is likely to catch fire.

Fastening a piece of wire netting over the top opening of the stove-pipe is another wise precaution; this acts as a spark arrester. When selecting a stove which is to perform service as a tent warmer, one may advisedly pay some attention to its dimensions in relation to those of the tent in which it is to be housed. In the case of a poor fit, a stove becomes very much in the way.

There is no such thing as perfection in a camp stove. When you have present in a certain stove an exceptional amount of business-like cooking efficiency, you sacrifice thereby varying degrees of attractive camp-fire romance. The very popular and extremely efficient gasoline stove is a case in point.

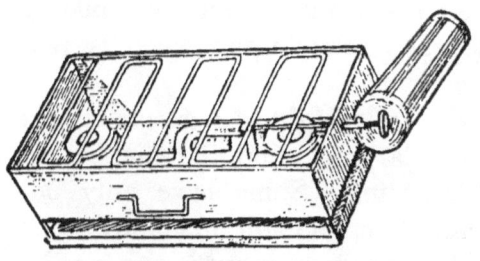

A FOLDING GASOLINE STOVE.

The gasoline stove is a great boon to motorists. The fuel is in the gasoline tank of the car and after this has been transferred by means of a small siphon to the gasoline tank of the stove, you have an intensely hot flame which is similar to that of a kitchen gas range. So far as speedy preparation of a hot meal is concerned, the gasoline stove is usually superior to the one of wood, for there is no waiting for the stove to become properly warmed. The hot flame is what does the cooking, and this is just as hot at the moment when it connects with a match as it will be ten minutes later.

Such a stove makes one quite independent both of fuel and weather conditions. During rainy weather the cooking may be done under cover and there is never the problem of wet wood with which to wrestle. A further advantage of the gasoline stove is that the risk of starting a forest fire becomes negligible. For this reason, there are some sections in which the camper who cooks with a gasoline flame is made welcome while the camper who depends solely upon wood is requested to move on.

The size and weight of a gasoline stove outfit is dependent largely upon the number of burners that it contains. Some have only one burner, others have two, and still others are equipped with three. The two-burner outfit seems to be the most generally popular stove of the lot. This is a suitcase-like metal box having a handle on one side by which it is carried. Although the stove is never heavy, you would not care to carry it very far by hand. It belongs essentially to motoring and motor-boating.

Sometimes a gasoline stove acts badly when you try to light it. As a rule this is because the burner is insufficiently heated. The burner of the type of gasoline stove that I have used most is equipped with a cup which you fill with gasoline and light before the gas is turned on. This preliminary flame is to all intents a torch which serves to heat the burner. The gas should not be turned on until the flame is almost burned out. Indeed, there are times when it is advisable to fill the cup twice before turning on the gas.

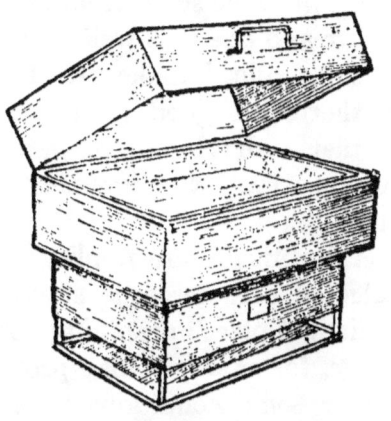

AN OVEN MOUNTED ON THE STOVE.

The gasoline stove has, to my way of thinking, two great drawbacks. One of these is the convenient tendency which it offers to specialize in fried food. This evil, however, may be overcome through the addition of a folding overhead oven which can be laid on top of the stove. Ovens are made which fit these gasoline stoves.

The second drawback of the gasoline stove is in its over-use. I have known campers to take long trips during which every meal from start to finish has been cooked over a gasoline flame. Not to know the spice and cheer of cooking at least an occasional meal over glowing wood coals is to miss a great deal. Food which is properly cooked over wood has an individual flavor which no other fuel of which I know can give.

I regard the gasoline stove as an excellent emergency measure and one that well earns its way on this score. As a rule, I make use of such a stove only when there is a good reason for doing so. For I feel that I should not be getting the best out of camping were I to eliminate the wood fire from the picture.

The same sentiments are applicable to various types of alcohol and kerosene stoves. Each of these has a distinct place in camping. An ordinary kerosene stove, for example, may prove a valuable adjunct under some conditions to a permanent camp. Or again, one finds it an advantage at times to carry "canned heat" as a precaution against either wet or scarce wood. Yet one would not care to cook exclusively by canned heat.

Some motoring campers carry with them both a gasoline stove and a wood-burning stove. There is more or less to be said in favor of such a combination. It need not weigh more than twenty pounds, and because of the folding proclivities of camp stoves these can be packed into a relatively small space. The increasing extent to which property owners in various communities have come to regard campers' wood fires with suspicion means that a burner stove such as the gasoline type comes pretty close to being a necessity so far as average motor camping is concerned. Besides, it comes in mighty handily during rainy weather.

CHAPTER XV

CAMPFIRE BAKING

A SAD tale of disillusionment is told of a youthful camper who emerged from a sporting outfitter's store with a brand-new shiny reflector oven under his arm thinking himself in possession of the latest invention of our progressive age. A few days later he exbibited his find to a venerable backwoodsman of seventy-five and started in to explain how it worked. He did not get very far.

"Shucks, son," interrupted the venerable, "my mother cooked with one o' them things when I was a boy and my grandma used one before her."

The reflector oven with which good housewives of Colonial times baked biscuits before blazing hearth fires is found to-day only in attics, antique shops, and museums; its need in the home ceased to exist when the modern kitchen range appeared upon the scene.

Yet, with camping, the case is different. Cooking over an out-of-doors wood fire may in numerous instances be a pretty close duplication of the hearth kitchen of a century and more ago. So far as these special conditions are concerned, there are probably no other baking utensils which are quite such a happy combination of convenience and efficiency as are the various modernized versions of the very old idea of cooking by means of reflected rays of heat.

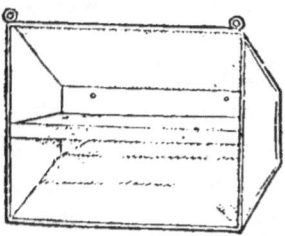

REFLECTOR OVEN BEFORE AN OPEN FIRE.

Twentieth-century reflector ovens are in general appearance and principle similar to those of the eighteenth century. They have, however, developed a convenient capacity for doubling into a very flat parcel when not being used, a custom which is regarded with favor by the heavily laden camper. The material of which these modern ovens are made may be of such various materials as aluminum, tin, tinned-steel plate, polished sheet iron and polished sheet steel.

Some of these ovens are so constructed that they may be attached to the side of a sheet metal stove (a possibility which never occured to our grandmothers), while others are essentially for use before the flames of a campfire. In case the oven is to be used apart from a stove, it is desirable that the metal of which it is made have an especially shiny surface which will readily reflect heat; preferably, aluminum or plated tin. Aluminum has the advantage of being light in weight, but plated tin is less expensive and more generally serviceable.

Not so bright a surface is essential in the case of the reflector oven which is attached to a stove. It should, however, have a polished surface. The material of the average oven made for this particular purpose is polished sheet steel, although almost any kind of reflector oven may be used in connection with a camp stove, provided, always, that it fits the side of the stove.

I will describe the use of a reflector oven placed either beside a wide-open campfire or facing the open end of a camp fireplace.

From your camping duffle you haul forth a metal package having the general shape and size of a roasting pan with the exception that it is only about three-quarters of an inch or an inch in thickness. This package, when unfolded and ready for use, is unlike any cooking utensil or probably anything else which you have ever seen.

Underneath, it has legs upon which to stand and above it has handles by which to be grasped, but as for the rest—well, perhaps one is minded of a very broad, wide-open mouth gaping at an open fire. The tongue is a horizontal shelf upon which rests the food that is to be baked or roasted. The top of the oven slopes back and downward like a roof, while the bottom slopes back and upward to meet it like a roof turned up-side-down.

The front of this peculiar oven is wholly open and faces the fire. The heat from the fire strikes the inner side of the sloping top and is reflected down upon the food. At the same time, heat strikes the inner side of the sloping bottom and is reflected upward upon the food. Thus even baking is assured. That is all there is to it; the polished metal reflects heat in very much the same manner that a mirror reflects light.

Such an oven is perhaps at its best when baking biscuits and bread. Bread making in camp life is sometimes a problem and this device, in case one has facilities for carrying it, offers a ready solution. The usefulness of the oven, however, is by no means confined to bread-stuffs. It will bake your potatoes, roast your meat, broil your fish, even cook pies, cakes, and puddings. When not being used for cooking, it serves as an excellent warming oven.

Successful cooking operations do, however, make certain demands. One of these is that the oven be kept polished and scarless. A second is that you build and keep burning the right kind of fire. The reasons, perhaps, are more or less obvious. With the front wide open, you have no great amount of confined heat stored away as in the case of an ordinary oven. Steady streams of reflected heat are what do the work. The efficiency of these streams should not be impaired.

Scratches upon the inside of the oven will lower its reflecting capacity to some extent while patches of rust and similar discolorations will do so seriously. The surfaces should be kept bright and shiny. Specs of soot from an open fire have an unkind custom of settling inside the oven during the process of baking and these should be wiped out as soon as the utensil cools. In doing so, be careful not to scratch the surfaces. Be careful also not to bend the oven in packing it.

The right kind of fire is important. In frying and broiling over a wood fire, we can never get satisfactory results by cooking with a blaze. We usually wait until the fire has died down to a layer of hot embers. In using the open reflector oven, however, exactly the reverse is true. In this case we need a steady intense wall of flame with the oven set ten or twelve inches distant. We must never jam the oven into the fire.

The flame should be fully as high and wide as the front of the oven and of equal intensity from top to bottom. If you have a flame which is only a few inches high, the greater part of the heat from this is confined to the lower section of the oven and the result will be uneven baking. The same may be true in some instances in case the flame towers to a point.

You will find well worth the effort some attention to method in obtaining a high, wide, and even flame, although the application of this is likely to vary. Thus, in case you use a reflecting oven in connection with the V-shaped type of log fireplace described in Chapter XIII, you are likely to find it advisable to stand the oven on the ground at the wide, open end of the V, facing the fire. Or in case the oven is to be used in front of a stone fireplace, build the fireplace sufficiently wide to permit the heat to creep around the ends of the oven. In some instances when a camp grate is made use of, it will be found worth while to pull a couple of flaming sticks from the fire under the grate and place these on top of it, thus adding to the towering result.

During the course of cooking with a reflector oven there are times when we wish as much heat as we can get without burning the food and there are other times when we wish only a moderate amount of heat. Kathrene Pinkerton wisely calls attention to the fact that the process of moving the oven backward or forward is a far more satisfactory means of regulation than is the manipulation of the fire.

A batch of biscuits, for example, needs to be started baking in a fairly moderate heat at a safe distance from the fire, but in due time it is advisable to move them up fairly close. The fire itself should be kept at the same intensity throughout

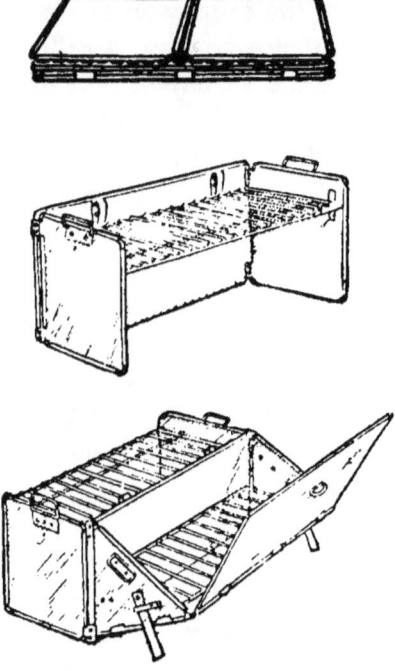

FOLDED, FRONT AND REAR VIEWS OF A COMBINATION SEMI-OPEN TYPE OF STOVE AND REFLECTOR OVEN.

the baking. The reflector oven does not function properly with a straggly fire.

When baking operations are well along, one usually finds it advisable to reverse the position of

Campfire Baking

the food so that the side of the food which has been nearest to the fire is away from it. In roasting a meat, one may profitably give this a preliminary searing in the frying pan.

In spite of the fact that the reflector oven demands a specified kind of fire, this does, as a matter of fact, dove-tail in most conveniently with the customary camp procedure of preparing a meal. First comes a blazing fire and over this we hang a kettle of water to boil. At this point we ordinarily are forced to wait until the fire dies down to embers before going on with further operations. Yet if in the meantime a reflector oven is propped at one side of the blaze and making the most of it, we are just that far ahead of the game. And we have hot biscuits for supper.

Folding reflector ovens which are sold in outfitting stores weigh variously from two to five pounds, range from twelve to eighteen inches in length and from eight to ten inches in width. In case you find it convenient to carry a package of these general dimensions and only about one inch thick, you have a simple, thoroughly practicable solution to baking problems.

Remarks in the foregoing paragraphs are especially applicable to the reflector oven in connection with its use either with a wide-open wood fire or an out-of-doors fireplace. They apply in a general way to the reflector oven that is attached to the side of a metal camp stove although not quite to the same extent. For example, care in having a certain kind of flame is not in this case so essential.

The reason for this is that when the reflector oven is attached to the side of a stove, it loses to some extent its character as a reflector. The cooking is now accomplished by means of confined hot air as well as by reflection. As regards the oven which is attached to a stove, there are obvious advantages to the type having a hinged top, for the food is hidden from view and you wish to open the top from time to time in order to watch its progress. When a reflector oven is used before an open fire, however, its front is always open, the food is in full view, and for this reason a hinged top is not essential.

In addition to the reflector oven, used either with or apart from a stove and the built-in type of oven with which some camp stoves are provided, there are, of course, several other baking methods practised in out-of-doors cooking. Some of these, heritages of natural resourcefulness from the redskin, gipsy, and backwoodsman, are described in separate chapters. The present chapter is devoted to baking tools commonly used in present-day camping.

Among these and thoroughly efficient at all times is the famous old Dutch oven. I doubt if

Campfire Baking

the lineage of the reflector oven is more ancient and honorable than that of this familiar cast-iron kettle.

Here is another very old idea which has persisted because it is a very good idea although the method is wholly different from that of the reflector oven. The method in this case consists either of baking or roasting the food between two layers of hot coals.

Some campers declare that you can bake bread better and roast meat to a more tender turn in

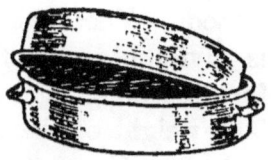

LEFT: A CAST-IRON DUTCH OVEN.
RIGHT: A "FEATHERWEIGHT" MODEL.

a Dutch oven than is possible with one of the reflecting type. In some instances, this may be so. I lugged a Dutch oven over a good part of the State of Utah one summer and I can bear witness to its high order of cooking efficiency. I can also vouch for its weight. This may range from ten to twenty-five pounds, depending upon the size of the oven. Which means considerably more of a burden than in the case of the reflector oven.

A Dutch oven is a cast-iron pot ranging from ten to fifteen inches in diameter and from about four to eight inches in depth, according to its weight and capacity. It is provided with a heavy, sunken, cast-iron lid, the object of this hollow lid being to serve as a receptacle for hot coals. The bottom of the oven rests upon another layer of hot coals raked to one side of the fire. The bread or meat within the oven is thus sandwiched between the two hot layers. As the coals die down, new ones are heaped on. The lid of the oven is provided with a handle and, by lifting this occasionally with a hook, you can follow the fortunes of the food. When baking bread in a Dutch oven, it is advisable that both oven and lid be quite hot before the dough goes in.

The weight of the Dutch oven is oftentimes a drawback. Campers who favor this method of baking, but who object to the carrying weight that goes with it, sometimes make use of a "featherweight" model of Dutch oven made of sheet metal. This weighs only about three or four pounds. Old-timers, however, will sagely assure you that you need the heavy cast-iron oven in order to get the best results.

Even though you never have cause actually to cook with a Dutch oven, you are pretty sure sooner or later to find good use for the idea upon which it operates. This principle of baking or

Campfire Baking 221

roasting between layers of hot coals is one which offers a number of convenient and valuable possibilities.

For example, when you go hiking, you are likely to find even the compact reflector oven too great a burden to be carried in your pack. But so long as you carry two dishes which are capable of standing strong heat, you have in these a Dutch oven of sorts.

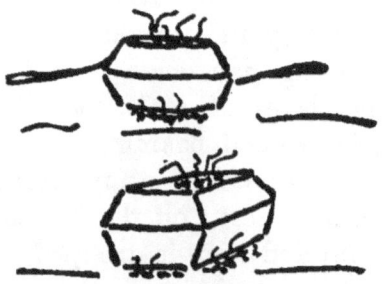

SHOWING THE USES OF TWO FRYING PANS AND TWO BAKING PANS AS OVENS.

The combination of a frying pan and a round, reasonably deep tin dish is a serviceable temporary oven. Rake a layer of coals to one side of the fire, place the dish containing the food on these, cover the food with an inverted frying pan, and put a layer of coals on top. Two frying pans, two plates, or two baking tins may each be used in the same manner. Or an oven may be made of two kettles, one smaller than the other, the larger being inverted over the smaller, bottom up.

Again, one may sometimes obtain pretty fair baking results by nesting a dish containing food within a kettle, covering the entire top with a lid and piling coals on this. Now and then you can pick up an old sheet of metal along the wayside and manufacture an oven of sorts. I once found a discarded wash-boiler in a trash heap and after turning it bottom-side up over a trench fireplace I had in it a roomy and workable oven.

A single frying pan, even devoid of a cover and its upper layer of coals, may, in some instances, perform good baking service. Thus in making some varieties of camp bread you can allow the crust to form on the bottom, then tip the pan on end and keep it propped in this position facing the blaze in much the same manner that the reflector oven is used.

Special types of ovens which may be used in connection with gasoline camp stoves warrant some mention. There are several different kinds of gasoline stoves, but the average and perhaps most generally satisfactory outfit of this sort consists of two burners which together with their working parts are housed within a metal box about sixteen inches long and ten inches wide. I am averaging the dimensions of a number of different makes.

Campfire Baking

There may be attached to the flat open top of this stove, above its burners, a sheet steel oven somewhat resembling a tin bread-box. This oven, as a rule, has the same general proportions as those of the stove, although it is a trifle larger. Thus with the oven set up, the heat from the burners traveling upward becomes confined within the walls of the oven and with this heat you conveniently can bake, roast, or broil. Various firms manufacturing gasoline camp stoves also make ovens which fit these.

Dr. Edward H. Williams, writing in *Field and Stream* makes the following interesting suggestions concerning the baking of frying pan bread on a burner stove without use of an oven:

Instead of investing five dollars in stove-metal, just invest five cents in an asbestos mat of the ordinary variety and mix it up with a little Yankee ingenuity in the bake-oven line. If you will put the asbestos mat over the grate of your stove so that the heat will be distributed and place an ordinary aluminum fry-pan with a tightly fitting cover on this, you will have an oven that will bake things to a turn in short order. It will not burn things either, if you remember to use a fry-pan made of aluminum and of no other metal. . . .

This oven will bake corn bread thoroughly in about ten or twelve minutes as against the ordinary oven's twenty. To be sure, the top of the bread will not be brown as in the other baker. But if you will tip your cover fry-pan wrong side up for about two minutes at the least, you will create a brown-topped Johnnie-cake.

I have tried the foregoing method with pretty fair results. It is a valuable point for either the gasoline or kerosene stove owner to remember. But it is hardly a method offering the same cooking scope as do the ordinary ovens which are especially designed for stoves of this sort.

More will be said concerning camp baking arrangements of various kinds in the chapter which follows.

CHAPTER XVI

FIRELESS COOKING

THE traditional "bean hole" that has been described with some detail in Chapter VI is an efficient camp application of the familiar principles of fireless cooking. The usefulness of the bean hole, as I have indicated, is by no means confined to the baking of beans.

Thus, before leaving camp in the morning for a day of hiking or fishing, you can give a savory stew its brief cooking start over a hot fire, bury it in the bean hole, and upon your return hours later have awaiting you a warm well-cooked supper. Or your breakfast cereal or fruit may cook slowly all night and be ready for breakfast. The principle involved is that of permitting the food to cook slowly by means of stored-up heat which gradually diminishes as the hours creep on; therefore, there is slight possibility either of burning or overcooking.

From the standpoint of convenience, there are obvious advantages under some circumstances in having a fireless cooker of the general type used ordinarily in the home, instead of the improvised hole-in-the-ground variety.

Some campers will find such a package, because of its bulk, distinctly inconvenient, but as regards permanent camps and also in the case of a migratory motor camper who has a large car or a trailer and hence plenty of room, it may prove quite practicable. For example, there are motoring campers who in the morning place food in a fireless cooker, put this in the car, travel all day, and in the meantime have their supper cooking.

A further advantage of the ordinary aboveground fireless cooker is that it may be used at other times as a means of keeping food cool. For both an ice-box and a fireless cooker are constructed upon the same principle, the idea being to retain respectively a given amount of stored-up cold or heat.

In using a fireless cooker, the food is heated over a fire until the cooking has begun and it is then placed in the fireless cooker. This is a tight vessel in which the food is completely surrounded by insulating material so designed that a minimum escape of the food's heat takes place.

Some foods are allowed to remain in a cooker for a longer period than are others, depending largely upon the nature of the food and its preliminary hot-fire start. The presence in some cases of an additional source of heat retention is another element that may cut down the cooking time; this usually takes the form of a hot piece of soapstone, brick, or iron plate. This extra source of heat corresponds in some respects to the hot ashes that are used in connection with the camp "bean hole" type of fireless cooker.

Elements of this nature should receive due consideration when either the bean hole or ordinary type of fireless cooker is used. It is obvious that in both cases, the term "fireless" cannot be taken wholly in a literal sense, for, in reality, a certain amount of fire plays an important part in the cooking. Ordinarily, the first stages of fireless cooking are identical with those of stove cooking.

Thus hominy grits are boiled for ten minutes before being placed in an ordinary fireless cooker, where they are allowed to remain overnight. Coarse hominy, on the other hand, requires forty-five minutes of boiling before being placed in the cooker. Rice, if given five minutes of boiling before being placed in the cooker, will be ready to be eaten in about an hour; because of the slowly diminishing heat. However, no harm will come to the rice ordinarily in case it is left in the cooker overnight.

The U. S. Department of Agriculture, in experimental work concerning the retention of heat in the process of fireless cooking, has placed boiling water (two hundred and twelve degrees) in a cooker and found its temperature after four hours to be one hundred and seventy-two degrees and after eight hours, one hundred and fifty-five degrees. Materials that are denser than water keep up a high temperature for a longer period. Hence, the density of a food is a further element that must be taken into consideration in knowing how long it should remain in the cooker.

The fireless cooker, of course, has its limitations. It cannot handle successfully food which requires a high dry heat for browning. Meats, however, may be partially roasted in the oven and finished in the cooker or begun in the cooker and finished in the oven. The fireless cooker is best suited to foods that require boiling, steaming, or long, slow cooking in a moist heat. The classes of foods best adapted to the cooker are cereals, soups, meats, vegetables, dried fruits, steamed breads, and puddings.

A meat stew is among the most successful of the cooker's accomplishments. This should be allowed to simmer over the fire for about a half hour before being placed in the cooker; it will be sufficiently cooked in about seven or eight hours. Less liquid should be put into any food to be prepared in a fireless cooker than in the case of a food cooked throughout over a fire; the food container being practically air-tight, there is slight opportunity for the water to evaporate.

Fireless cookers are used quite extensively in camping, which is small wonder, for they are

Fireless Cooking 229

peculiarly well suited to this purpose. Not infrequently they are camp-built affairs fashioned from materials at hand. The Department of Agriculture in one of its bulletins gives a clear and instructive account of how to make a fireless cooker of this general sort. I will give a brief summary of the information contained within this bulletin. Of course, you can always buy a ready-made fireless cooker, but there may come a dull day in camp when it strikes your fancy to manufacture your own.

The materials needed in the construction of a fireless cooker are:

A box or some other sort of outside container such as a small barrel, butter tub, or tin pail.

Some good insulating and packing material.

A kettle with a tight-fitting lid for holding the food.

A container for the kettle or a lining for the nest in which the kettle is to be placed.

A cushion or pad of insulating material with which to cover the top of the kettle.

For the outside container referred to, a tightly built wood box is perhaps the most satisfactory device. A box having the dimensions of about fifteen by fifteen by twenty-eight inches offers sufficient space to accommodate two cooking vessels. This size is advisable in case bulk is no object. A single-vessel size, however, is sometimes more practicable for campers who motor. Whatever the size of the container, it should be sufficiently large to allow for at least four inches of packing material all around the nest in which the kettle is placed.

An advantage of the two-kettle arrangement is, that small amounts of food cannot be cooked very satisfactorily in a single large kettle. Two smaller kettles are rather better. It is important that the covers of the kettles fit on tightly. The size of a kettle may be determined by the amount of food to be cooked; the six-quart size is convenient for general use. Enameled-ware kettles are satisfactory and so are aluminum vessels. Tin and iron cannot be recommended. It is possible to buy kettles that are made especially for fireless cookers.

The cooking scope of the fireless cooker becomes more extensive if it is provided with an extra source of heat, as previously indicated. Thus, a soapstone, brick, or iron plate is heated and placed in the nest under the kettle. Sometimes an additional hot stone is placed over the kettle. Extra heat is a help although not essential. Its presence introduces a possible danger from fire as regards inflammable packing material. To avoid this danger, a metal lining must be provided for the nest in which the cooking kettle and the hot stone are placed.

Fireless Cooking

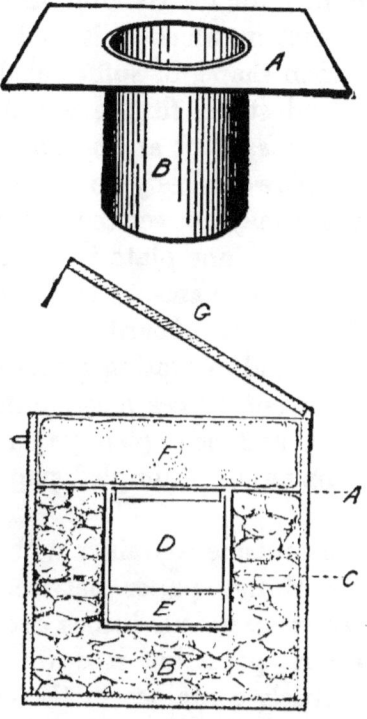

HOW TO MAKE A FIRELESS COOKER.

Above: Metal lining for nest of fireless cooker. *A*, rim to cover packing material. *B*, metal container for cooking kettle and hot stone.

Below: Longitudinal section through fireless cooker, showing details of the construction. *A*, outside container (wooden box, old trunk, etc.). *B*, packing or insulating material (crumpled paper, cinders, etc.). *C*, metal lining of nest. *D*, cooking kettle. *E*, soapstone plate, or other source of heat. *F*, pad of excelsior for covering top. *G*, hinged cover of outside container.

The container for the cooking kettle or the lining for the nest in which it is to be put should be cylindrical in shape, of sufficient depth to hold both kettle and stone, fit the vessel with a fair amount of snugness, but at the same time the latter must be allowed freely to move in and out. A metal bucket may answer the purpose. In case neither a hot stone nor plate is to be used in the cooker, the fire risk vanishes and the lining may be made of strong cardboard.

For packing and insulating material, the choice of a variety of substances may be made, such as hay, excelsior, and crumpled paper. Of these inexpensive materials, crumpled paper is perhaps the best.

To pack the outside container with paper, crush single sheets of newspaper between the hands. Pack a layer at least four inches deep in the bottom of the box, pounding it down with a stick. Stand the kettle's container in the center of this four-inch layer and pack more paper around it, as solidly as possible and up to its top. The box should lack about four inches of being full of packing material.

A cushion or pad must be provided to fill completely the space between the top of the packing and the cover of the box. This may be made of some heavy material, such as denim and stuffed with cotton, crumpled paper, excelsior, or hay.

Fireless Cooking 233

And this operation completes the construction of a serviceable fireless cooker.

Let us return now to the more primitive camp bean hole. A hole in the ground is always available; and apparatus such as has just been described is not in every case available. As a matter of fact, so far as variety is concerned, a hole in the ground offers a wider range of cooking methods than does the carefully constructed fireless cooker. I have said that the term "fireless" cannot be accepted literally in either connection, and although a bean hole is essentially a fireless cooker in principle there are times when it also may become a baking oven.

In case you require speedier results than in slow fireless cooking, you can keep a hot fire going above the hole while the food underneath is being cooked. The trench type of fireplace, which I have described in Chapter XIII, serves as a single example of how a very fair loaf of bread may be baked in such a hole.

Before baking operations begin, a fire is kept going in this trench for nearly an hour in order thoroughly to heat it; then the hot coals are raked out and laid on top of the sheet metal lid. The bread is placed in the trench through its open end and the end is tightly closed. The subsequent amount of heat may be regulated largely by the amount of fire that is kept going on top. It is

234 Camp Grub

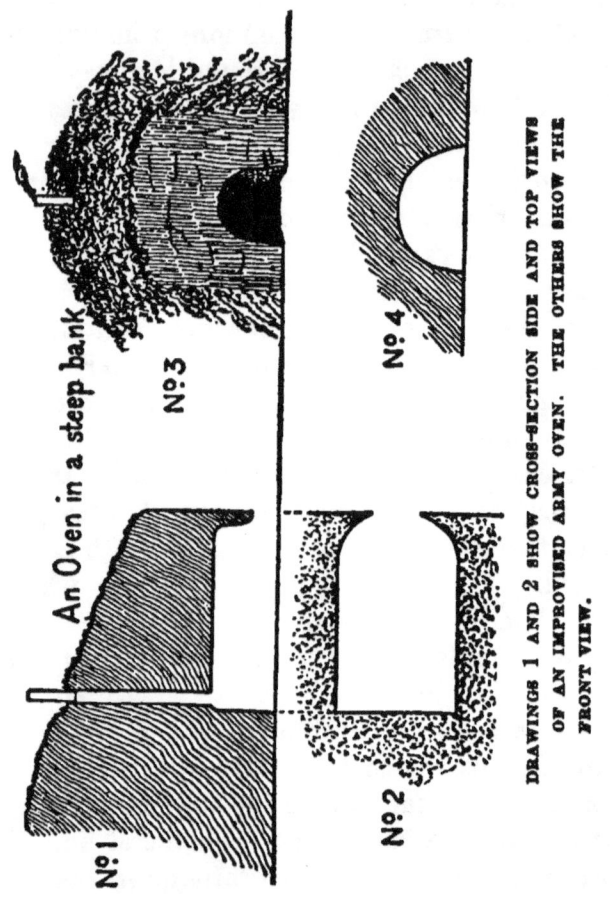

No. 1 An Oven in a steep bank
No. 2
No. 3
No. 4

DRAWINGS 1 AND 2 SHOW CROSS-SECTION SIDE AND TOP VIEWS OF AN IMPROVISED ARMY OVEN. THE OTHERS SHOW THE FRONT VIEW.

Fireless Cooking 235

possible to have in such an oven, heat which closely approximates that of a kitchen range oven.

Various types of improvised clay ovens, made use of by the United States Army during field service, are indicative of the varied cooking possibilities of a hole in the ground. One of these consists of a hole dug horizontally into the side of a steep bank after a vertical face has been cut in the bank. The driving of a stake into the bank higher up leaves a hole which serves as a flue. A piece of stove-pipe may be planted in the ground at the upper end of the hole.

A possible modification of this type of oven is a right-angled excavation about two feet wide in the bank, the vertical face in this case being the back of the oven instead of its front. Thus three sides of the oven automatically are complete. Two flat rocks placed horizontally a foot or so apart become respectively a baking shelf and the top. The fire is built on the ground under the shelf. A third flat rock, set on edge, becomes the door of the oven.

The Army two-barrel clay oven is an ingenious device which when slightly modified in size sometimes proves of value in general camping. This is built upon a form consisting of two empty sugar barrels laid end to end on level ground, then covered with a two-inch layer of wet sand.

Next you mix some clay with hay or grass,

giving a stiff mixture, and mold over the sand a layer of this varying from eight inches in thickness at the bottom to four inches at the top. This is allowed to stand for a day or two and then another three-inch layer of clay is added. Throughout this construction, one end of the oven remains entirely open, but the other end is sealed, with the exception of a small vent which is left for the draught.

The oven is allowed to stand a day longer and then the barrels inside are set afire, care being taken not to burn these too quickly, for an intense fire at this stage may cause the whole structure to cave in. After the barrels are burned out, the sand is scraped from the top and sides and removed. The oven is now complete.

The foregoing is designed to serve a large number of men. As regards general camping purposes, it may be modified accordingly in its construction. A single small barrel or even a lard pail may perhaps supply ample oven space. Sometimes it is advisable to bury the barrel partially in the ground (on its side) and later fashion a crude chimney of some sort on the upper side.

Various improvised ovens such as have just been described, ranging from the bean hole to the barrel affair may perform either fireless cooking or baking service, depending upon the manner in which one regulates the heat. And proper regulation of heat as applied to some of these crude improvised devices, in common with many supposedly simple primitive methods of cooking, is not always so simple as it may sound. One learns only by experience and usually spoils a fairish amount of good food in the process. But still, it is worth the learning.

CHAPTER XVII

KEEPING FOOD FRESH

THE increasing use of fresh foods in camping has brought with it added need for keeping one's food supply cool. The great amount of dependence that is placed upon a home kitchen refrigerator during warm weather may cause one to wonder what sort of substitute for this valuable device is available in camp life.

As in many other matters concerned with camping, much depends upon how and where one goes. As a rule, both the traveling motorist and the permanent camper are in a better position to keep food fresh than is the wilderness hiker on the march. Yet in practically all cases, ready cooling facilities are available. Even the hiker with his limited supply of fresh food may keep a jar of butter fresh by carrying it wrapped in a wet cloth.

In case you camp permanently in one spot and have an ice supply available but are lacking in a refrigerator of any sort in which to keep it, you may improvise one. A hole in the ground is almost invariably the most successful type of improvised

Keeping Food Fresh 239

ice-boxes. The following instructions, taken from a U. S. Army manual, may prove of value:

To provide a simple ice-box for the field, sink a packing box of suitable size into the ground and prepare a close-fitting cover in two parts for convenience in handling. It is well to surround the box with heavy paper or with packed straw or grass to prevent dirt from falling in through the cracks.

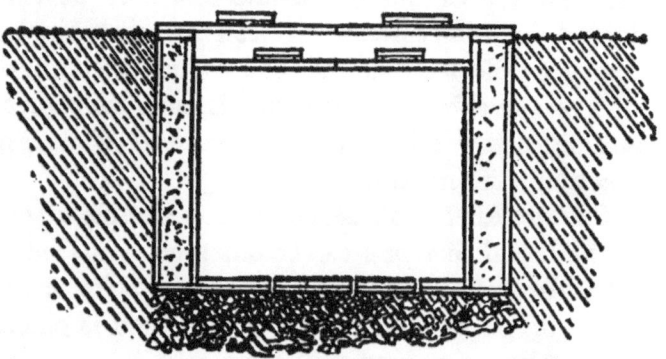

CROSS-SECTION VIEW OF AN IMPROVISED HOLE-IN-THE-GROUND ICE-BOX.

To provide drainage, bore several holes in the bottom of the box and if practicable put a quantity of stone or gravel in the bottom of the pit before installing the box. If facilities are at hand, provide a double box. It will be more cleanly and on account of the double top, the ice will last longer.

The foregoing is sound in principle and may be adapted to individual needs as conditions warrant.

The double-box arrangement referred to is, without doubt, the best. In making use of this arrangement, however, I have found it advisable to lay four or five fair-sized rocks on the bottom of the outer box in order that the inner box may be slightly raised, thus giving an air space underneath.

Ice is not always available when one goes camping. In a good many instances it may be considered an unnecessary as well as unobtainable luxury. Cold water is the food-cooling medium of the average camper. And this is both convenient and peculiarly effective. The variety of its application is interesting.

The fireless cooker serves as an example of one of the less direct phases. If hot food is placed in a fireless cooker, this will remain hot for many hours; or, on the other hand, if cold food is placed in a cooker, the food will stay cold. Insulation in the apparatus prevents the escape of the cold. It is essential, however, that the food be chilled before it is placed in the cooker.

Vacuum bottles of various sorts operate upon the same principle. At the close of Chapter XI, mention has been made of the ice-box possibilities of a vacuum food jar.

I have found by lining an ordinary tin breadbox with corrugated paper and then in turn covering the box with canvas, that jars of food

Keeping Food Fresh 241

previously chilled in spring water will remain cool throughout a day's motor run. This method perhaps is not so effective as an ice-box, fireless cooker or vacuum food jar, but it indicates the ease with which food may be kept cool when some slight amount of thought is given to the matter.

A canvas water bag of the type that keeps water cold by means of slow and steady evaporation through its weaves is part of the equipment of many campers. Thus a water-filled bag of this sort may readily be carried while motoring. And few more effective methods of keeping either a jar of butter or milk cool can be found than by carrying the jar in the water.

Recently, an ingenious camp outfitter has applied the water-bag principle of slow evaporation (which keeps the water temperature low) to a small rectangular type of running-board ice-box. The convenient result is an ice-box that keeps things cool without ice; water does the work. The interior of the box (this is entirely dry) offers carrying space for a considerable amount of food. Although the inner wall of this unique ice-box is metal, its outer wall is canvas; the water is in between and slowly seeps out through the canvas.

Capillary attraction is another natural law for which many campers find good use in keeping their food fresh. Try the following experiment some time and you will see how effectively this may work. Place a basin of water on the table, and in this immerse one end of a long piece of cloth. By gradual stages the entire piece will become wet and remain wet as long as there is water in the basin. Furthermore, it will be cool, for both evaporation and capillary attraction take place.

You will see how readily adaptable this is to camping. Thus food may be confined within a bucket, a basin of water placed on top of this and a gunnysack or old piece of blanket draped so that it covers completely both basin and blanket. The cloth may be held down in the water by a rock.

Various adaptations of this principle may be used. One of these, applicable to permanent camping, is described by P. C. Kangieser in *Field and Stream,* under the title "Iceless Refrigerator for the Camp." This consists of four corner posts and various cross-pieces resulting in a framework that is a trifle less than four feet high and one and one-half feet wide. There are three shelves, small sticks slightly separated being used for this purpose. Mr. Kangieser's further instructions are as follows:

Place around the frame, mosquito netting, so it will completely cover all sides as well as the top and bottom, and arrange it so there is a flap at the front similar to a tent flap so it can be thrown back to the side to gain access to the inside; sew a piece of tape around the edges of the netting at

Keeping Food Fresh 243

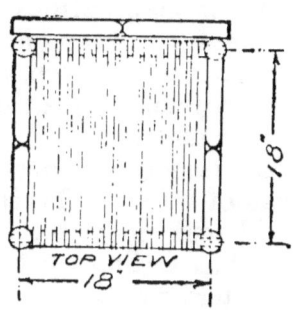
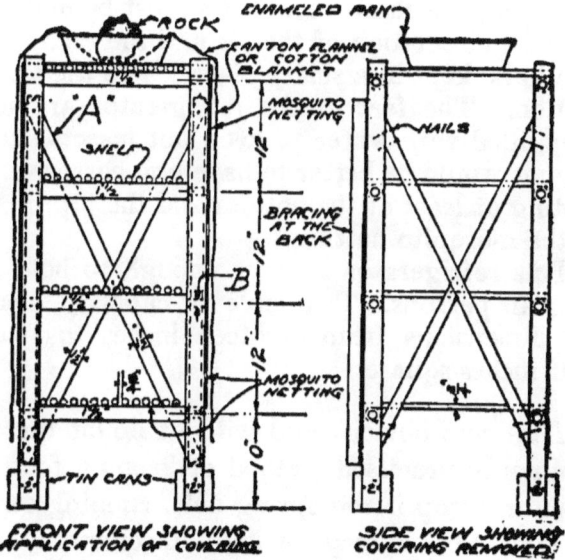

Courtesy of "Field and Stream."

DETAILS SHOWING CONSTRUCTION OF "ICELESS REFRIGERATOR" DESCRIBED IN TEXT.

the flap, and sew snap buttons every three inches for secure fastening to keep out the flies.

After the netting has been applied, a cover is made of canton flannel or an old cotton blanket and is hung around the frame over the netting; the ends are extended up over the top into the enameled pan of water. This serves as wicks and the water will soak down the cloth and keep the cover moist; thus setting up an evaporation and keeping the interior cool.

The cloth should be white, as that refracts heat and light, the shelves and sides must be built open to assist circulation of the air and the refrigerator should be kept in a shady place where the air is in motion. The feet of the refrigerator are set in cans filled with water to keep out insects such as ants; it would be better to have non-corrosive wire netting at least at the bottom and the top, instead of the mosquito netting.

This refrigerator is large enough to hold food for four persons. To double the capacity, increase the dimensions from eighteen inches to twenty-four inches square.

The most obvious and without doubt the most commonly practised method of keeping food cool when in camp is the spring hole, running stream, or lake. Food may be kept uncommonly fresh by such means, especially so in case it is confined within jars which may be completely submerged.

If camping close by a spring, it is usually advisable to dig out a small hole just below the

Keeping Food Fresh 245

spring, fix this up a bit with rocks, cover, and so on, reserving it exclusively for the purpose of keeping food cool. The hole-in-the-ground icebox idea previously described may offer suggestions in this respect, although in this case there is no need for ice.

Lake water being quite a few degrees warmer than spring water, it is not always very satisfactory. In some instances, however, there are springs in a lake within a few swings of the paddle from shore, as one quickly discovers while swimming. Lacking other facilities for keeping food fresh during warm spells, one may sometimes benefit by these unseen springs. One may sink the food.

The most satisfactory way of going about this is to tie a long rope in the form of a loop after this rope has been threaded through a small loop attached to a rock anchor and through the hole in a float. The anchor is dropped to the spring and then a bag containing watertight food jars is attached to the rope and lowered to the anchor; the same general idea as two buckets in a well.

Likelihood of being able to locate an unseen spring in the lake when you need it is rather less than more; this method of keeping food cool is not generally practicable. A small pit dug in the shore close by the water usually serves very well, for underground water is of lower temperature than is surface water, and even though you do not dig down to water level, the earth in such a spot is quite cooling.

Various cooling methods described in the foregoing serve to indicate that if through choice or necessity you are forced to get along without ice, there can be readily devised an effective substitute.

A UNIQUE TYPE OF PORTABLE ICE-BOX USED EXTENSIVELY BY MOTOR CAMPERS.

But this does not alter the fact that ice when available is a very pleasant adjunct to camping. Furthermore, the presence of a portable ice-box in one's camping equipment is in many instances quite feasible. This is especially true of motor camping.

Many of the portable ice-boxes carried by motoring campers are the results of their own resourcefulness in the form of making use of an old bread or cracker tin in a new guise. Although these appear to serve passably well. it is unques-

Keeping Food Fresh 247

tionably true that a box that has been originally designed to hold ice, does better. The most efficient portable ice-box is one having double walls with either dead air space or some sort of insulating material in between; in other words, one of the same general construction as that of a well-made home ice-box.

Camping outfitters sell various portable ice-boxes of this sort. Some of these are clamped to the running-board of a car, while others are provided with handles and can be placed in the tonneau or wherever in the car they will be least in the way. In fact, before considering any kind of an ice-box for a camping trip, you should be reasonably sure that it will not become a burden.

CHAPTER XVIII

PURE DRINKING WATER

MOST city dwellers are not called upon ordinarily to give thought to the importance of pure drinking water. Efficient engineers do the thinking for them; health is automatically protected from the ravages of disease by highly specialized water systems. But when the city dweller goes vacationing, the situation is oftentimes different. He should always bear this in mind and be guided accordingly.

How is one to know that one's drinking water is pure? The only way of knowing with absolute surety is through having it analyzed. So far as the average camper is concerned, an analysis of the water is an impractical proceeding.

A simple rule-of-thumb water test sometimes used in the open is as follows: A small quantity of water having a temperature of about seventy-five degrees is placed in a bottle and shaken up and down for several minutes; then you remove the cork and smell the water. In case there is an unpleasant odor, this means that the water is unfit for drinking purposes. One must not lose sight

Pure Drinking Water 249

of the fact, however, that water may sometimes contain typhoid germs and not smell badly even with this test.

Another common test, perhaps more reliable, consists of placing in the water which is under suspicion, a few drops of a weak solution of permanganate of potash. An ounce supply of these tiny lavender colored crystals lasts for more water tests than one probably will ever have cause to make. A few of these go a long way. They are a poison and should be handled with care.

The usual proportion in making the solution is one part permanganate to one thousand parts water. This solution is of a rich pinkish-lavender color and after a few drops of it are placed in the water which is to be tested, this acquires a light pinkish tinge. The test revolves about the permanency of this. In case the pinkish tinge presently vanishes, this indicates that the water is unfit for drinking. But if the color remains, the water is regarded as being reasonably safe. Remember, always, that permanganate of potash is a poison.

Neither of the two foregoing tests may be considered as being accurate. They are of some practical value in camping in that they may give a rough idea of the relative virtue or iniquity of a water supply when more accurate means of acquiring that information are lacking. But they do not alter the fact that the out-of-doors person who travels afield, sipping strange water supplies every here and there, is through necessity taking chances that cannot be helped.

One must, to some degree, take these chances. But the element of chance is always greatly minimized in case one goes fortified with definite knowledge of what to look for and what to look *out* for in relation to drinking water.

The gravest danger from polluted water is eliminated if, before starting upon a vacation trip, you are vaccinated against typhoid. This method of immunization is very simple and extremely effective; surprisingly enough, comparatively few campers take advantage of it. Even this immunity, however, does not necessarily eliminate intestinal disturbances which may be the result of drinking polluted waters containing germs less fatal than typhoid. Every one should "watch one's step" when approaching strange drinking water.

The terms "pure" and "impure" as applied to natural water supplies are wholly relative terms. In reality, all natural waters are to some extent impure. According to the strict definition of the scientist, we must be content with water which is "impure." And so long as we keep on the safe side of a somewhat vague border line that spells danger and disease, the more of this we drink, the better for our health.

Pure Drinking Water 251

We must be careful, however, not to cross the line. Waters that harbor decaying vegetation, such as swamp waters, are across the line, while those waters that have become contaminated either by human or animal filth are of a most injurious degree of impurity. In other words, we must drink what is commonly called "pure" water.

Wells, springs, streams, and lakes are the most usual sources of drinking water supply in which you are forced to place your trust during a vacation. In each case, the purity may be relatively high or relatively low depending largely upon surroundings. The appearance of the water itself is not always a safe guide; sparkling cool water having the appearance of being very pure may in some instances be dangerously polluted. On the other hand, there are some waters which, while most objectionable to the eye, are in reality of a relatively high degree of purity.

We would become exceedingly thirsty were we to wait until we arrived at the perfect water supply. The best that we can do as a rule is to average up the conditions which we find at hand. The surroundings of a certain well or spring are likely to serve as a reasonably accurate index to the relative virtue or iniquity of its waters.

Cast your eye here and there about the premises and make mental notes of points in its favor and disfavor. In case the average turns out to be exceedingly low, you would do wisely to pass on to a well or spring offering a higher average.

Consider the farm-house well. The well of a deserted farm-house should never be trusted under any conditions; in frequent cases it serves as a receptacle for various sorts of filth and dead animals. As regards the farm-house well from which people are drinking constantly, the fact that it is being used is, of course, a point in its favor. Likely as not, a motoring camper could travel the width of the continent drinking periodically from such wells without any harm coming to him. But then, again, one bad guess might prove disastrous.

In spite of the fact that a well is being used constantly, it may in some cases be obviously unsanitary and under such conditions should be passed by. Polluted water is extremely debilitating even though it neither contains typhoid germs nor sends a person to a sick bed. During the course of a sanitary survey made in one of the New England states some time ago, sixteen per cent of one hundred and forty-seven shallow wells which were examined showed evidence of sewage pollution. Many campers, no doubt, have unknowingly sipped water from wells of this general sort without suffering any noticeable ill effects. But it hasn't done them a bit of good.

Contamination which pollutes a well comes originally from the surface of the ground. It may

Pure Drinking Water 253

seep in through the top of the well or it may seep through the earth, even from quite a distance away. When you come to a well which your judgment tells you is safely removed from any underground contamination and which is so thoroughly well curbed and tightly covered that the possibility of seepage from above is slight, you are reasonably safe in drinking its waters.

In case the drainage from the house is toward the well, it is distinctly in the questionable class. But perhaps the most outstanding example of the well which should be left severely alone is the one which is the recipient both of surface and underground drainage from latrine and stable. This type is by no means uncommon in country sections.

Our forefathers may have been good farmers, but in some instances they proved themselves mighty poor sanitary engineers. They can hardly be blamed for picking the lowest level in sight for the digging of a well, for this meant ease in reaching water. Unfortunately, however, this spot not infrequently was the barnyard. Dr. Harold B. Wood makes the statement that any well which is located in a barnyard is always contaminated.

The drinking-water supply, which is commonly regarded as being the purest of all, is the spring. In some cases this confidence in the spring is well founded, while in others it is open to question. As a general rule, the waters of a spring, if taken directly from the spot where they bubble out of the earth or if piped from this spot, are of a higher degree of purity than are those of the average well. The spring which is far back in the woods, especially in a hilly section, is almost invariably of unquestionable purity.

Yet, after all, the main point of difference between a spring and a well is that the former is a natural outlet for underground water while the latter is an artificial outlet. This means that in a settled section, a spring may be subject to much the same suspicion as a well. In both cases, a natural filtration process takes place which to varying degrees purifies the water, but this process is not always so effective as it is popularly supposed to be. With the spring, as in the case of the well, you must size up the surroundings and use your judgment.

Another common belief long since disproved by science is that the running water of a surface stream always purifies itself. It does, no doubt, to some extent, but this hardly alters the fact that in the average farming community the sparkling waters of a pleasant winding brook are likely to be tragically polluted. Even in instances where there is no visible sign of contamination, there is likelihood of the presence of unhealthy surface drainage from cow pastures and barnyards. Never drink from a stream that further up may be bordered in any way by human habitation.

The most recent findings of sanitary engineering seem to indicate greater drinking safety in standing lake water than in the case of a running stream, the reason for this being that in the former instance the purifying rays of the sun have a better opportunity to kill disease germs. This safety does not apply, of course, to ordinary small ponds rank with vegetation or large lakes polluted with sewage. As human settlement increases, the danger of disease in like proportion increases with it. A great deal of questionable lake water is made pure by means of mechanical purifying processes. But I am speaking of natural water supplies from the standpoint of the needs of the average camper.

Away back in the wilderness beyond human habitation almost all waters, with the exception of those which are rank with rotting vegetation, are relatively pure. You can, as a rule, drink with perfect safety from spring, lake, or stream. Possibly it is rather an unfortunate commentary upon the habits of human beings that this should be so. The relative impurity of water invariably increases with the coming of settlers. And when choosing any waters for drinking purposes, this is the main element to be kept in mind—the chance of pollution by human habitation.

Dr. Claude Fordyce recommends for camping purposes the use of a chemical preparation known as "Halazone," saying that when one of these tablets is added to a quart of water and allowed to stand for twenty minutes the water is rendered harmless.

I do not wish to appear to be a calamity howler in this matter of drinking water. But it really is a most important element in a vacation. Ordinarily, a camper does not have to look far in order to find good water, but on the other hand it is sometimes wholly unavailable. In case the water is at all subject to suspicion, there is a simple method of making it absolutely harmless. This is by boiling it for twenty minutes. It does no good merely to allow it to simmer; the water must actually boil for this period.

Some campers make use of small filter pumps having somewhat the appearance of a bicycle pump. These clarify the water and thus make it more appetizing, a point worthy of note as regards muddy water. These pumps, however, do not rid the water of germs. Boiling is the only readily available facility which will do that. Boiled water ordinarily has a rather flat taste, the reason being that the boiling process expels all air from it. The air returns and the flat taste is absent if after boiling you pour the water several times from one vessel to another.

Pure Drinking Water 257

Whenever one makes camp and depends upon a natural water supply of any sort such as a nearby spring for drinking water, a great amount of importance should be attached to the location of this spring in relation to that of the latrine. The two must be widely separated; the possibility of water pollution both by means of surface drainage and underground seepage should be rigidly guarded against.

The topographical formation of the ground usually serves as a fairly accurate guide in this respect. Underground seepage as a rule is parallel to surface drainage. Thus if a latrine were located at a slight elevation above a spring although quite distant from it, the dip of the land toward the spring might in some cases be the means of carrying pollution to the water.

Underground as well as surface water is likely to take the shortest and quickest route to water which is located at a lower level. One finds no great difficulty in reading the meaning of natural conditions when one is on the lookout for them. The great danger comes from not stopping to figure out simple points of this sort.

A pure drinking water supply should in every way be kept pure. A spring ordinarily must be cleaned out about once a week, for unless this precaution is taken, vegetation forms which to a limited extent impairs the purity of the water.

The fresh, clean appearance of the water immediately after a spring has been cleaned out, and then becomes filled up again serves as an indication of the value of the cleaning.

Ordinary surface drainage into the spring should be guarded against so far as possible. Even a small trench and clay mound fashioned along the top and sides of the spring will to a great extent prevent the entrance of undesirable washings from the bank above. A cover is a further safeguard.

Either a wood tank or a barrel spring which in addition to being safely covered is provided with a small pipe outlet usually serves one with water having a higher degree of purity than in the case of a spring which lacks such protection. A cement tank, of course, is better still. The advantage of the pipe outlet is that it prevents the more or less constant dipping in of unclean cups and pails.

The construction of a wood tank enclosing a spring is no great task. Campers who remain for a long time in one place are likely to find the work quite worth while. Such a tank should be cleaned out from time to time.

There should never be any confusion when camping as regards the location of the water which is used for drinking purposes and that in which dishes, clothes or one's person are washed. The

Pure Drinking Water

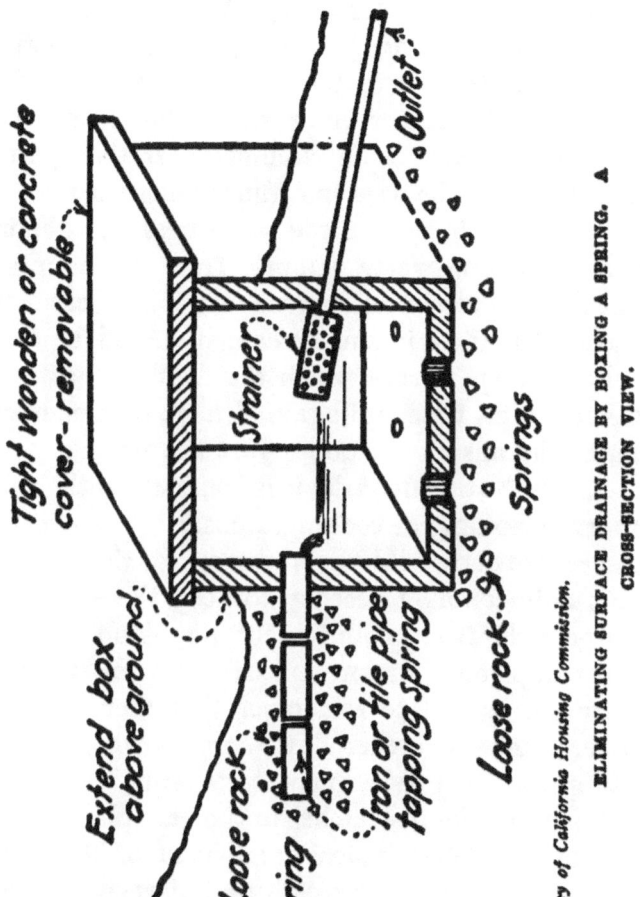

Courtesy of California Housing Commission.

ELIMINATING SURFACE DRAINAGE BY BOXING A SPRING. A CROSS-SECTION VIEW.

British Army, I have been told, makes it a practise to plant a certain colored flag at the edge of water that is for drinking purposes; a flag of another color at water where the men may wash, and a flag of still another color where the horses are watered. Under some circumstances this system might perhaps be used in ordinary camping.

When one is back in the wilderness and obtains one's drinking-water supply from a mountain stream, it is rather an obvious fact that in case any washing is done in this stream it should be done below the spot from which the drinking water is taken. Yet, time and again, I have seen campers make the mistake of doing just the reverse.

In the National Parks it is contrary to the rules to wash clothing or cooking utensils in the streams. As regards any wilderness waters, for that matter, it is only common decency to keep these as clean as possible from pollution of any kind. When one camps on a stream and uses this for drinking water, it is well to remember that there may be other campers further down stream who also are using it as their drinking-water supply.

There are long stretches in the vast plains country of the West which are devoid of drinkable water. Hence the necessity of carrying water. Touring motorists are perhaps the largest class of campers affected in this respect and fortunately the transportation of a reasonably generous sup-

Pure Drinking Water 261

ply is fairly simple. When spanning an alkali or desert stretch of country, it is advisable to have five gallons of good water on hand at all times.

A CONVENIENT METHOD OF ATTACHING A WATER BAG TO A CAR.

A large semicircular canteen attached to the running-board of a car is a convenient device for carrying water. But the most generally satisfactory arrangement, perhaps, is the famous canvas water bag. This water container has played an important part in pioneering history and it is equally adaptable to present day camping needs.

A bag of this sort must be soaked thoroughly before being used and it should be carried in such a position that it does not rub against the car. Lashings from the top of the bag to the car body and from the bottom of the bag to the outer edge of the running-board is a convenient arrangement.

Canvas water bags are made in various sizes ranging from one to five gallons. Two smaller sized bags are sometimes more suitable than is one large bag.

CHAPTER XIX

KEEPING YOUR CAMP CLEAN

WHEN people go camping there not infrequently ensues an unfortunate tendency toward a let-down from their customary high standards of cleanliness and sanitation. This may apply both to personal cleanliness and that of the camp.

Perhaps one neglects to wash one's hands before sitting down to a meal, becomes careless of the disposal of tin cans and garbage, permits disease-carrying flies to breed freely, washes but partially the cooking utensils, tosses greasy dish water upon the ground close by the living quarters. These and similar actions are contrary to ordinary rules of good health—rules which are quite as applicable to camp life as they are to city life—in some cases more so.

One gains nothing by choosing a camping site which is sanitary unless one keeps it sanitary. With the exception of fully equipped camping grounds, first attention after the choosing of a site should ordinarily be given to the digging of a latrine. Any defilement of the surface of the ground is an offense for which the uncivilized savage may perhaps be pardoned, but which should never be tolerated in civilized man. A small, easily packed shovel having a folding handle should be part of the equipment of the camping motorist.

The primitive trench latrine, the sort with which the average farm-house is provided, is at its best an unsanitary device. Any campers who remain permanently in one place and have at hand facilities for the construction of a more sanitary method of sewage disposal such as the septic tank or even removable metal cans should take advantage of these facilities.

Unfortunately, the primitive trench latrine is the sole method which the average camper finds available. So it is that one must make the best of the situation by using an extreme amount of care as regards the condition in which the latrine is kept. To slight any precaution is to court sickness. Some towns that provide camping grounds for motorists are open to severe criticism because of the disgracefully unsanitary condition in which they permit latrines of this sort to remain. But for that matter, so are the campers open to criticism.

Whenever practicable, the latrine should be located at least two hundred feet from the living quarters and fully that distance from the water supply. Of these two elements, the greater amount of importance is attached to its position in relation to the water supply. As I have indicated in Chapter XVIII, the possibility of water pollu-

Keeping Your Camp Clean 265

tion both by means of surface drainage and underground seepage must be rigidly guarded against.

With the safety of the water supply assured, the next step is that of safeguarding the latrine against flies. These vile insects are a very real danger. As regards any "here to-day and away to-morrow" camping party, the latrine which is dug may be merely a shallow trench. Every time this trench is made use of, shovelsful of previously excavated earth should be returned to it.

Campers who remain for a week or more on one site should employ added precautions. The longer one stays, the greater the precautions must be. The information which follows concerning the growth and habits of flies may serve as some indication of why this is so.

A fly lays from seventy-five to one hundred and twenty-five eggs upon the surface of breeding material. During midsummer, the eggs hatch in anywhere from twelve to twenty-four hours and then in a period ranging from ten to fourteen days, the result is a swarm of grown-up disease-carrying flies. A report made by Harold Farnworth Gray in the Transactions of the American Society of Civil Engineers as applied to sanitation in construction camps is of interest to all campers. Mr. Gray says:

It has been proved conclusively that under such conditions as are usual in camps, flies may be gross transmitters of such diseases as typhoid, dysentery, and various intestinal disorders. During the Spanish-American War when more soldiers were killed by disease than by bullets, large numbers of flies were often observed in the mess tents, the bodies and feet of them being whitened by the lime in the latrine which they had recently visited. It may be stated almost as an axiom that the sanitary condition of a camp varies inversely as the number of flies present.

The fly risk as regards a trench latrine becomes greatly minimized in case every available precaution is taken in the way of keeping its contents covered with lime, dirt, or crude oil, and whenever practicable (as in a camp of long duration) keeping various openings to the trench screened and banked with earth. Remember that the trench latrine is a seventeenth-century device which must be regarded from a twentieth century sanitation viewpoint.

Rotting garbage is another fly risk. This is applicable to all kinds of kitchen waste, including greasy paper, the solid matter in dish water, skins of vegetables, and emptied tin cans. Any available decomposing matter irrespective of how small it may be serves as an invitation which flies rarely fail to accept.

Some people innocently cast emptied tin cans into the brush at one side of a camp, thinking that so long as there is nothing directly under one's

Keeping Your Camp Clean 267

eyes and nose which offends sight and smell they are keeping their camp in sanitary condition. As a matter of fact, specks of food that quickly decompose almost invariably remain in an emptied can and these attract flies. In addition to this shortcoming of the empty can, it becomes half filled with water after the first rain and thereby serves as an ideal breeding container for mosquitoes.

When kitchen waste is made inaccessible to flies, these pests cease to breed. Elimination of breeding material is far more effective than all the screens in the world. Garbage and other waste may be eliminated in two ways: by burying it and by burning it. Fire is the most effective destroyer of undesirable matter and in all cases where this method is practicable it should be used. If facilities for the disposal of waste by fire are lacking, you can dig a hole and bury it. But in doing so, keep an eye upon the drinking water supply.

A small camping party that is constantly on the go may use an ordinary campfire as an incinerator. Tin cans as well as garbage are tossed into the consuming embers. A tin can, from the fly standpoint, becomes thoroughly harmless after it has been licked by fire, but even so may breed mosquitoes unless it is buried. Bury the remnants of all tin cans before breaking camp.

The campfire becomes a more serviceable incinerator in case it is built upon a pit-filled collection of loose stones. In Chapter XIII, I have briefly indicated one method: the digging of a pit about twenty inches deep, two or three feet wide, and about three or four feet long, and filling this to the surface of the ground with loose stones. The ends

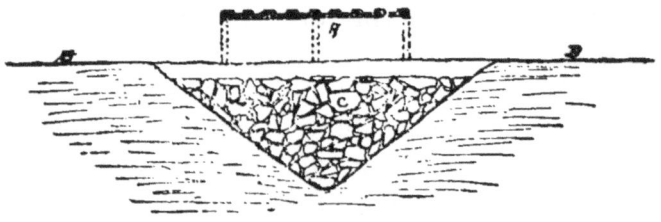

Courtesy of "Outing."

CROSS-SECTION PLAN OF CAMP FIRE AND INCINERATOR.
A, Fire jack. *B*, Surface of ground. *C*, Broken stone in pit.

of the trench may either be vertical or slope toward the center like a basin. The fire blazing on top of the stones thoroughly heats them. Thus, the liquid part of garbage upon trickling through the hot stones evaporates, while the solid parts are burned by the fire.

A simple incinerator of the foregoing type does very well for a party of three or four people who are camping for a number of days or weeks in one site. After being used for a reasonably long time, it should be filled in, for eventually it may draw flies. Another pit may readily be dug.

Keeping Your Camp Clean 269

An improvised type of incinerator used by the U. S. Army during field service is a much better device for camps of some size, in which there is

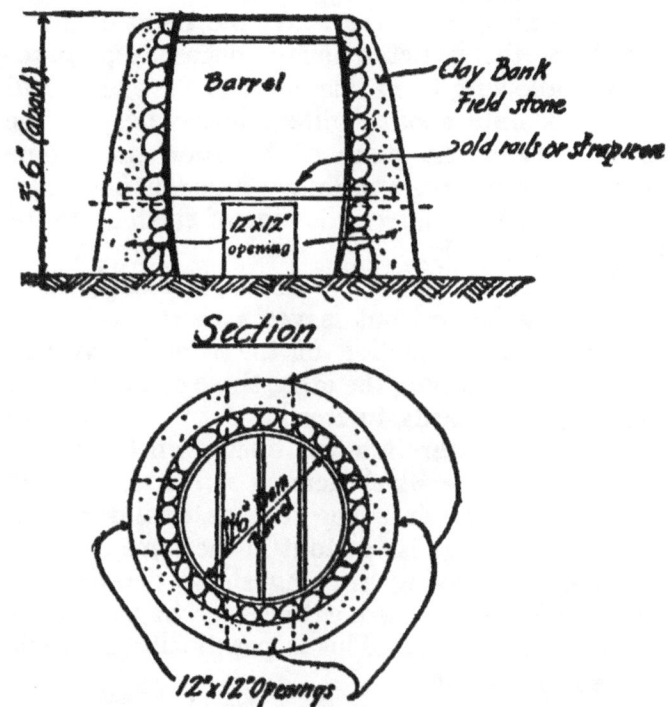

Courtesy of California Housing Commission.

THE BARREL TYPE OF INCINERATOR. SUITABLE FOR A LARGE CAMP.

a considerable amount of kitchen refuse to be burned, say, in a camp ranging from fifty to one hundred people. I will give the following details of construction as they appear in a U. S. Army manual:

Dig two trenches ten feet long and twelve inches wide bisecting each other. At the point of bisection have the trenches thirty inches deep, gradually shallowing from this point to the ends. Fill with rock until about eighteen inches deep at the center. Over the place of bisection place four boards to support an ordinary sugar or flour barrel. Around the barrel pile sods of earth up to the top. Pack tightly.

Make a fire in the trench under the barrel, which upon being burned out leaves a hard cone. According to the direction of the wind, leave one trench open and plug the other three openings near the cone with boards, turf or loose soil. This gives a draft of air through the open trench and up through the cone which acts as a flue. . . . The fire is kept up by dropping fuel material down the cone, and garbage is fed to it in the same manner.

An accompanying drawing shows details of a barrel incinerator used extensively in California construction camps. This is practically the same as the Army device.

The common camp practise of tossing broadcast, pans of liquid kitchen waste is not to be commended. Surface ground which is slimy from the grease of many pans of dish water is neither pleasant nor healthy ground. The place for dish water

Keeping Your Camp Clean 271

is under-ground. Both types of incinerators described in the foregoing may serve as receptacles in this respect.

In case the garbage is to be buried instead of being burned, kitchen waste of all varieties may be relegated to a pit dug for the purpose and then in turn covered with a layer of earth.

These layers of earth quickly fill the pit. Therefore, instead of being under the necessity of digging a new pit every day or two, it is sometimes more convenient to have a single pit which may be used for a fairly long period. This may be accomplished without the addition of dirt in case the interior is made tight against flies. You cover the hole with boards, leaving a small trap door in the center through which the waste is poured. If boards are unavailable, sticks may be used. It is usually advisable to bank the covering with earth.

The opening in the top of the pit should be provided with a removable box-sieve of wire screening which in turn is surmounted by a removable cover. This double precaution serves as a reasonably safe measure against the entrance of flies. The darkness of the pit is a further advantage in this respect. Flies are not ordinarily attracted to dark places; they like the light. The depth of a pit may depend largely upon circumstances. When dug in a clay soil, it should be of greater depth than in the case of a porous soil. And care should always be

272 Camp Grub

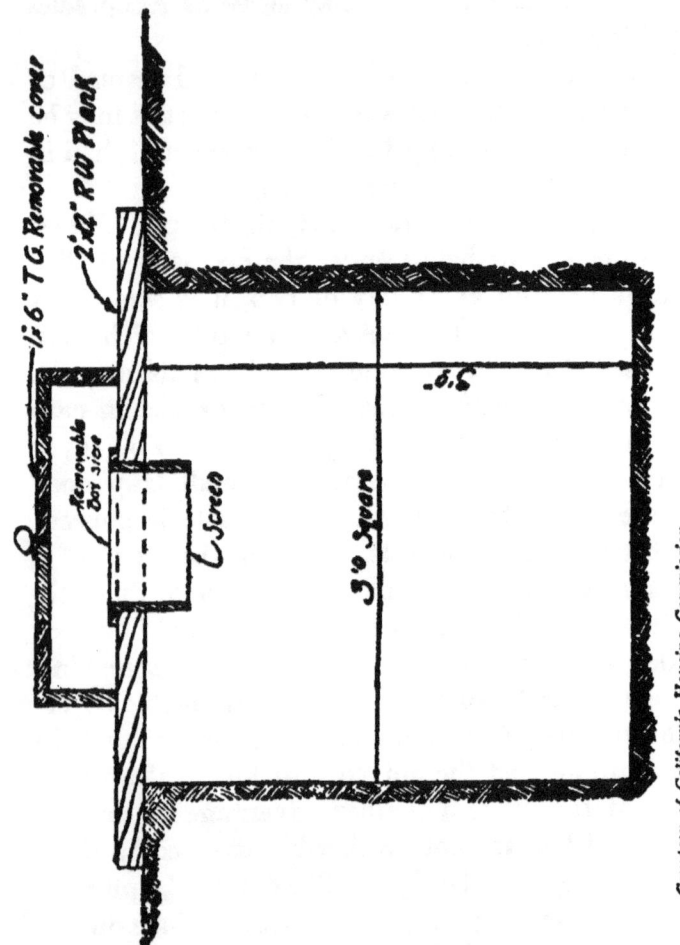

Courtesy of California Housing Commission.

CONSTRUCTION OF A CAMP KITCHEN SEEPAGE PIT.

Keeping Your Camp Clean 273

taken to have it a safe distance from the drinking-water supply.

As a receptacle for all kitchen waste, such a pit cannot be used indefinitely. After a time it becomes unsanitary and then should be filled in. Fire is the most effective method of disposal for waste. As a matter of fact, the most sanitary manner of making use of a pit of the sort just described, is in confining its service to liquid waste such as dishwater. In this case, the liquid may be poured through the box-sieve and any solid particles remaining on top may be burned in the fire.

Camping conditions vary and with these their needs. One's own good judgment is the best guide as to when precautionary measures such as the foregoing are needed or not needed. Ordinarily, for a brief stay and few campers it is sufficient merely to throw the garbage into the campfire and pour the dishwater into a small hole in the ground. The garbage, however, must be totally exterminated and the dishwater hole filled. And don't neglect to bury the remnants of tin cans.

Last but not least, camp cooking and dining dishes should be kept scrupulously clean. In this element perhaps to a greater extent than any other is there a tendency toward a let-down from one's usual high standards. Utensils sometimes have the appearance of being clean when in reality they are quite unsanitary. The common camp practises of swashing out a pan with cold water and moss or jabbing a fork into the earth have some value in that they take off outer layers of grease. But they don't go far enough.

There is only one way of having dishes really clean and sanitary, this being a liberal application of soap and very hot water. There is also a method of having one of the least attractive phases of camping (I won't say a joy) but at least, unobjectionable. This is by setting water to heat over the fire while the meal is in progress. The longer one puts off dishwashing, the more difficult it becomes to tackle. But with boiling water ready at hand when the meal is finished, the chore is dispatched with surprising speed and no longer seems drudgery.

THE END

www.ingramcontent.com/pod-product-compliance
Lightning Source LLC
LaVergne TN
LVHW041622060526
838200LV00040B/1395